RESEARCH FOR
SOCIAL JUSTICE

RESEARCH FOR SOCIAL JUSTICE

A Community-Based Approach

Adje van de Sande & Karen Schwartz

Fernwood Publishing
Halifax & Winnipeg

Editing: Brenda Conroy
Cover design: John van der Woude
Printed and bound in Canada by Hignell Book Printing

Published in Canada by Fernwood Publishing
32 Oceanvista Lane
Black Point, Nova Scotia, B0J 1B0
and 748 Broadway Avenue, Winnipeg, Manitoba, R3G 0X3
www.fernwoodpublishing.ca

Fernwood Publishing Company Limited gratefully acknowledges the financial support of the Government of Canada through the Canada Book Fund, the Canada Council for the Arts, the Nova Scotia Department of Tourism and Culture, the Manitoba Department of Culture, Heritage and Tourism under the Manitoba Publishers Marketing Assistance Program and the Province of Manitoba, through the Book Publishing Tax Credit, for our publishing program.

Library and Archives Canada Cataloguing in Publication

Van de Sande, Adje, 1949-
Research for social justice : a community-based approach /
Adje van de Sande, Karen Schwartz.

Includes bibliographical references and index.
ISBN 978-1-55266-441-4

1. Social service--Research--Methodology. 2. Community-based social services. 3. Social justice. I. Schwartz, Karen, 1955- II. Title.

HV11.V34 2011   361.3072   C2011-902777-1

Contents

Acknowledgements

The completion of this book would not have been possible without the help of a number of people. We would like to thank our family members for their support and encouragement, including our partners, Mary Ann Jenkins and Ian Schwartz, as well as Taylor Jenkins for her excellent work in editing the final draft. Colleagues and students have also provided invaluable help, especially Bessa Whitmore, who originally designed the community-based research course at Carleton University and has been an ongoing source of inspiration. Amanda Watson, one of our graduate students, helped with a very thorough editing of the initial manuscript. And finally we'd like to acknowledge all of the students in the research and evaluation course over the years who have lent us their voices in the many quotes that we included in the text. Thanks also to the people at Fernwood Publishing: Wayne Antony for publishing this book; Beverley Rach for page design and layout; John van der Woude for cover design; Debbie Mathers for pre-production; and Brenda Conroy for copy editing.

Preface

Since 1997–98, Carleton University School of Social Work has structured the master of social work research course so that students in small groups engage in research with community agencies. This book draws heavily from our experiences as instructors, from over a hundred research projects carried out by our students, and from the feedback from organizations that have benefitted from these research projects. With permission, we have also made extensive use of student projects to illustrate the concepts presented in this text. Over the years, the course has evolved, and we have tried as much as possible to be true to our structural roots.

The book is intended for social work students engaged in community-based research who wish to follow a structural approach. However, the book will also benefit social workers who are increasingly called on to conduct research such as program evaluations and needs assessments within their organizations. Lastly, social science students, broadly engaged in social justice and community-based research, will find this book a useful guide.

Truth in Facts?

Qualitative vs. quantitative
 hasn't really ever been a question for me;
   it's been the former, hands down, before the latter
   in life – experientially.
      I'd rather trust "truths" not facts,
      personal stories, not cold hard stats;
         For numbers are used, man-i-pulated,
         so that any, and all(?) conclusions stated—
            even with peer review and scientific certainty—
      are only as good as their Theories' qualities.

And since theories change,
 with the whims of people, church and state
   popular opinion, pocket books
   and sometimes factual debate—
      To truly know how things are turning
      (it's now earth round the sun, sun around what… we're still learning!)
         takes one on one deep understanding,
         self-reflection, and self-commanding
            reflexive participatory engaging communication
            not factual numeric categorizing qualifications.

      So to enable a knowing of what truly counts,
               what is quality;
         to account for the differences defined
            by every you and me;
         to ensure the use of all knowing to create
             a just society:
         we must see beyond the quantifiable
               to our shared humanity

b!WILDer2010
(Used with permission of the poet, Beth Schilling)

1. Research as Politics

For the last several decades, social work curricula have included research as a required course at both the undergraduate and graduate levels. Despite ongoing concerns about the perceived gap between research and practice (Rubin and Babbie 2008), some authors (Marlow 2005; Yegidis, Weinbach and Morrison-Rodriquez 2009) attempt to minimize the gap by showing how the two follow similar steps. Most social work research texts emphasize the importance of following the scientific method as the most effective way to obtain trustworthy information (Royse 2008; Rubin and Babbie 2008; Yegidis, Weinbach and Morrison-Rodriquez 2009; Faulkner and Faulkner 2009). The traditional scientific method requires the researcher to strive to be neutral, objective and free from the influences of society. While we agree that certain aspects of the scientific method should be maintained, we do not believe that social work research should be value-free. Just as social work is committed to social justice and social change, that should be the aim of social work research. We argue that social work research should be carried out from a structural perspective and follow anti-oppressive practice (AOP) principles. The structural perspective views the problems experienced by people as rooted in the social, political and economic structures of society. We also believe that schools of social work have a responsibility to leave the "ivory tower" and stay connected to the community. Besides the usual method of having students do their field placements in the community, schools could provide a valuable service by having graduate social work students engage in community-based research.

Structural Social Work

The term "structural" originated in the United States in the 1970s. Middleman and Goldberg (1974) introduced the structural approach as a way for the social worker to intervene "to improve the quality of the relationship between people and their social environment by bringing to bear, changing, or creating social structures" (32).[1]

The structural approach in practice and research is based on a "conflict" perspective of society, which, within sociological literature, is one of two competing perspectives of how society functions (Mullaly 2007). The "order"

The Martin Fields Research Project

This project illustrates research based on a structural perspective, which was carried out by MSW students. This type of research provides students with real, hands-on experience while at the same time offering an important service to community organizations.

Martin Fields is a social housing community owned and managed by Ottawa Community Housing, the city's largest housing provider. The residents are mostly low-income families, people on social assistance and recent immigrants to Canada. The physical space consists of 150 row houses and two community buildings, a portable and a community house. Space in the community house is used for recreational, social, cultural, and educational programs. The Ottawa West Community Health Centre (OWCHC) provides a large portion of the funding for the community house.

The research project was undertaken to assess community capacity in order to provide the community house with useful information to help in future program planning and funding proposals. The intention was to encourage community member participation in the management of the community house and to enhance the connection among residents and community house staff. The research team, made up of five MSW students, invited community members to act as advisors in the development of the research. In summary, there were four objectives for this research project: 1) to include community members as a significant part of the research process; 2) to provide a snapshot of the demographics of the Martin Fields community; 3) to explore what the community wants and needs from the community house; and 4) to explore and share strengths and good news.

This research was conducted in two phases. In keeping with a participatory framework, Phase 1 engaged community members as research advisors. Semi-structured interviews with these advisors informed the content, format and administration of the research instrument, a questionnaire, which was administered to willing participants of the Martin Fields community in Phase 2. Recruitment for Phase 1 was carried out with the assistance of the community house coordinator, who personally contacted potential community advisors. A recruitment flyer in four languages (English, French, Somali and Arabic) was also posted at the community house.

The community advisors addressed issues about the focus of the research and provided input on the choice of questions on the survey instrument. The draft questionnaire was presented to the board of the community house, which included such stakeholders as community residents, representatives of the OWCHC and the Food Bank, and which provided additional input into the survey instrument.

For Phase 2, a multi-lingual flyer was delivered to each mailbox. This flyer indicated the date the door-to-door surveys would begin and invited interested participants to visit the research team at the community house during two scheduled periods. Additionally, community advisors were asked to spread the word about the dates and times of the survey. Prior to beginning the study, the research team had also visited the community on a few occasions to attend community events. This allowed them to introduce themselves and to engage in casual conversation about the project. Finally, the research project, complete with pictures of the team, was featured on the front page of the community newsletter. Since residents of the Martin Fields community spoke a range of languages, the team made use of language interpreters to assist with those participants who spoke neither English nor French. Team members visited individual units at various times during the day. If there was no response, a blank survey form was left in the mailbox.

While community advisors were not involved in the data collection or the analysis of the data, they helped decide how to disseminate the research results. Suggestions from advisors included delivering a flyer door-to-door with a summary of the key findings and performing a slide presentation to the tenant's association at an open meeting.[1]

Note

1. We have not used the real name of the community house to protect the identity of the participants, but we have permission to use this document from the relevant community health centre; 2011.

perspective, consistent with neoliberal ideology, posits that society is basically functioning in an orderly fashion, characterized by stability and consensus. This perspective views social problems as being caused by individuals who do not respect the rules of society and who need to be taught to follow these rules (Reasons and Perdue 1981). According to the conflict perspective, in keeping with social democratic and Marxist ideology, the more powerful groups in society are able to pursue their own self-interests and oppress others through coercion and subjugation (Mullaly 2007).

While mainstream social work focuses primarily on the individual and maintaining social order (Payne 2005), structural social work takes the conflict perspective and focuses on oppressive social structures. As Bob Mullaly (2007: 22) explains, mainstream social workers are asked by the state to "police the casualties of unemployment, inflation, economic neglect and policies that place private profit above human need." Therefore, structural social work research should expose the effects of an exploitative and alienating social order and create a picture of individual and group experiences of stigma and discrimination. Thus, a structural approach "seeks to change the social system and not the individual who receives, through no fault of their own, the results of defective social arrangements" (Mullaly 2007: 245).

To show how the structural approach is integrated into social work practice, Moreau (1989) identifies the following five practice methods:

1. Defence of the Client

Social workers using the structural approach help to defend their clients against an oppressive system. Quite often, clients are not familiar with their rights and require someone to advocate on their behalf. This includes writing letters, attending meetings and, if needed, subverting agency policy. Ensuring that clients are aware of their eligibility for resources and how to access these resources is a final aspect of client defence (Schwartz and O'Brien 2010).

2. Collectivization

It is common for clients to feel that the problems they face are the result of their individual shortcomings. They need to know that they are not alone in their struggles. An important role of the structural social worker is to connect clients to support networks and reduce their isolation and alienation. To illustrate collectivization, Colleen Lundy (2004: 64) provides an example of a group for incest survivors, with the worker using educational material such as other women's stories about incest and survival to help her clients accept that it is not a "private shame."

3. Materialization

A cornerstone of the structural approach is the materialist analysis. Many of the personal problems experienced by clients are a direct result of material deprivation. A single parent on social assistance will often struggle with depression and feelings of inadequacy. Rather than focusing on the mental health issues, social workers help clients make the connection between their poverty and their mental health concerns and realize that they are not to blame for structural problems beyond their control.

4. Increasing Client Power in the Relationship

Clients coming for assistance typically experience feelings of powerlessness. Part of the work of a structural social worker is to increase the power of clients in the worker-client relationship by clear contracting, avoiding jargon, sharing rationales behind proposed interventions and showing clients what is in their files. Instead of solving the client's problems, the worker helps clients understand their situation in such a way so as to mobilize their own energy to find solutions. In this way, clients see themselves as in control of their own problems and the possible solutions.

5. Enhancing the Client's Power through Personal Change

Without judging or blaming, the structural social worker maximizes the client's potential for personal change of thoughts and behaviours that are self-destructive or destructive to others. This is done by focusing on clients' strengths, offering a range of possible alternative behaviours and helping them make the connection between their thoughts and behaviours and their social context.

4

We can also relate Moreau's practice methods to research. Hick (1997) believes that structural social work can inform researchers to view social problems as located in social structures and relations and in the dominant neoliberal ideology rather than in the individual, couple or family. For instance, with respect to materialization, researchers have long found a strong correlation between poverty and mental illness: the lower a person's socio-economic status the greater their chances of suffering from mental distress. Recent studies have shown that poverty, unemployment and lack of affordable housing can precede a diagnosis of mental illness and psychiatric hospitalization and are, therefore, causal factors (Hudson 2005). Helping clients acquire decent housing, employment, adequate food and so on is extremely important in the prevention and relief of mental distress. Many mental health service users find their experiences of stigma more disturbing than the suffering from mental illness. Large-scale studies that document this discrimination can be used in the process of collectivization to help clients understand that they are not alone in experiencing discrimination (Schwartz and O'Brien 2010). *Out of the Shadows at Last* (Kirby and Keon 2006–1) is a Senate report that documents, among other things, the stories of people with mental health problems who have experienced discrimination. This document led to the creation of the Mental Health Commission of Canada, which is formulating a national mental health policy. It was also used to advocate for the increased inclusion of mental health service users in policy formation.

Generally, involving clients at all stages of the research process is one way of empowering them. This practice is an integral part of a structural research method called participatory action research (discussed in Chapter Six). Critics of traditional forms of research feel it is important that the values of participant empowerment and conscientization are reflected in structural forms of research (Brown and Reitsma-Street 2003). As an example, if an organization is requesting a needs assessment, the researcher would ensure that clients are involved in the research process. This way, the organization becomes aware of what clients feel they need and has the opportunity to be more responsive. Furthermore, it is empowering for clients to see their ideas reflected in the wording of a questionnaire and their voices included in the final research report. In research carried out through the University of Calgary, nine people diagnosed with schizophrenia participated in every aspect of a study that investigated housing for people with psychiatric disabilities. In the video *Hearing [Our] Voices* (Everett 2007), they eloquently describe the impact that being involved in the project had on their self-esteem, sense of agency and ability to engage in research: "Our voice together is a lot more powerful than if we had been just one person doing a project"; "I really learned something. I've gained something and enriched my life"; "We are all consultants now. People ask us for our opinions."

Anti-Oppressive Practice

As stated earlier, in addition to a structural perspective, social work research should follow anti-oppressive practice principles. AOP is an umbrella term that includes a number of social justice oriented approaches, such as feminist, Marxist, post-modernist and structural to name a few. Many AOP principles relate directly to research. Donna Baines points out: "Social work is not a neutral, technical profession, but an active political process" (2007: 21). As discussed earlier, where the scientific method and most mainstream social work research texts emphasize the importance of being as neutral and objective as possible, we argue that social work research should not be neutral; it should actively pursue social justice and social change.

Another relevant principle from AOP is that "participatory approaches between practitioners and clients are necessary" (21). A participatory approach to research means that subjects of the research should be actively involved in all phases, including the choice of research questions, the development of the methods and data-gathering instruments, the analysis of the data and the preparation of the final report. This approach presents some difficult but not insurmountable challenges for social work students, who are subject to rigid university ethics regulations.

A third AOP principle is that "social work needs to build allies and work with social movements" (21). Chapter Five, on research partners, discusses researchers' need to identify the relevant partners in the research project, including those who may be directly or indirectly oppressing people, as well as those who may become potential allies in the project and who will support the change process. A fourth AOP principle states that "a blended-heterdox social justice perspective provides the best potential for politicized, transformative social work practice" (22). What this suggests is that social work researchers should use a mixed methods design, including methods that are not typically used in mainstream social work research such as ethno-methodology. A final AOP principle that relates to social work research is that "self-reflexive practice and ongoing social analysis are essential components of social justice oriented social work practice" (22). We need to become aware of our own deeply integrated beliefs about what constitutes good research and which research paradigm we are naturally inclined to follow, as most of us have been heavily influenced by the empiricist approach to research. The following is an excerpt from a student journal:

> When I studied Anti-Oppressive Practice and Research, I engaged in reflexivity and extensively explored how my worldview was impacted by my social location as a White, able, "straight" person of western European descent who is mid-twenties, from a middle-class background and who grew up in traditional Coast Salish territory, also known as Victoria, B.C. I believe researchers,

like all persons, have worldviews that are formed by the way they were socialized based on their social location and lived experiences.[2]

A good part of students' anxiety towards and conflicted feelings about research may be because they do not see the connection between practice and research. Since the 1970s, social work educators have challenged the profession to prove that their practice was effective (Fischer 2009). Early studies found several difficulties with casework practices, including service users not being actively involved in their own cases and not agreeing with practitioners on the goals of intervention. There was evidence that social work education did not adequately prepare practioners and that social work practice was not effective. This led to the demand for schools of social work to provide training in research methods and for social workers to engage in evidence-based practice. Evidence-based practice in social work (EBPSW) is defined as "the planned use of empirically supported assessment and intervention methods combined with the judicious use of monitoring and evaluation strategies for the purpose of improving the psycho-social well being of clients" (O'Hare 2005: 6). It is clearly important that social workers reflect on and find ways to evaluate the effectiveness of their practice. However, service users have been telling social workers for some time that the traditional EBPSW model practices, developed through research clinical trials,[3] is deficient because it does not accept certain types of evidence, such as service users' perception of care (Manderscheid 2006). Consequently, models for examining practice based on values that are more consistent with those of structural social workers have emerged, for example, practice-based evidence. This model allows for the co-construction by the social worker and the service user of evidence of how well interventions work.

Instructors need to help social work students see research as an effective tool to challenge oppression. Reflexive exercises can help students understand how their worldview and personal theoretical perspective are relevant not only for practice but research as well. Research questions, methods of data collection and ways of interpreting data need to be consistent with their theoretical analysis. "Only by knowing that oppression is a social construction can social work embark on a deconstruction of oppressive practices and reconstruction of society characterized by true social equality" (Mullaly 2007: 284).

The following is from the reflexive journal of one of our MSW students as she describes her thoughts as a woman of colour and struggles with the power dynamics within her research team:

Feminist research proponents state that the researcher cannot be distanced from the research process. As a woman of colour,

> I always feel the presence of my identity in my social work practice as a woman and as a person of colour. My struggle in this research is the degree to which I will be able to bring this identity in to this research process. Among a number of group members involved in this study, I am the only woman of colour, more specifically a black immigrant woman. My experiences of marginalization on the basis of this identity are such that my views in various groups among mainstream members have not been valued or validated. As a result, I wonder how much say I will have in the process. I also wonder how much of this self-awareness will limit my openness to other people's ideas. This makes me weary of the group power dynamics that may play out and how my own experiences and biases regarding my identity will influence my participation in this research project.[4]

By being open about her concerns, this student can assist her team members in confronting their own prejudices. This reflexive statement does not leave the "white students" off the hook because they are also engaging in their own process of self-reflection.

Conclusion

This chapter introduces the basic principles underlying community-based research carried out from a structural perspective. We believe that such research is more in keeping with our core social work values, which are to challenge oppression and work towards social change. The next several chapters explore how these principles should inform research. In addition to topics such as research paradigms and ethics, this book also looks at participatory action research. PAR is very much in keeping with the structural approach, and the material covered in that chapter is key to a comprehensive understanding of the approach.

Research conducted from a structural perspective can be both quantitative and qualitative. However, regardless of the choice of research design, it is important for social work researchers to be clear with organizations that the research will be conducted from a structural perspective. Organizations will need to agree to the structural and anti-oppressive principles that researchers intend to follow. Not all organizations will support the structural approach, and this may limit available research opportunities. On the other hand, it is hoped that most organizations will see the long-term benefits of this approach for their clients in terms of contributing to meaningful change.

DISCUSSION QUESTIONS
1. What are some of the challenges in conducting research from a structural perspective?
2. Do you believe that participants have a role to play in the development and implementation of the research? Explain.

3. What do you think the relationship between research and practice should be?
4. Have you encountered research projects or research results that have led to social change?

Notes

1. Maurice Moreau (1979) and his colleagues at the School of Social Work at Carleton University in Ottawa further developed the structural approach based on feminist and Marxist principles. Since then, it has been known as the "Structural School" (Lundy 2004). Work on the structural approach continued with Bob Mullaly publishing a series of three books (1993, 1997, 2007), which provided a comprehensive framework for the approach.
2. Christine Howey, Reflexive Journal, April 2011.
3. Traditionally, the gold standard of research has been clinical trials. This means quantitative studies that employ a control group not exposed to a treatment compared with a group exposed to a treatment.
4. Concillia Muonde, Reflexive Journal, November 2007.

2. Research Paradigms

The dominant approach to research in the West has been and continues to be the scientific method, which is associated with what is called the modernist or positivist paradigm. However, recent decades have seen a growing shift toward what is called post-modernism, post-positivism or interpretivism (Marlow 2005; Rubin and Babbie 2008). Thanks largely to the contribution of feminists, many now acknowledge that objective and value-neutral research, as upheld by the positivist, empiricist view, is a myth (Harding 1987; Smith 1987; Tanesini 1999). Yet, in spite of the increased acceptance of interpretivism, social work is still heavily influenced by the scientific method, as defined by positivists. For instance, Bonnie Yegidis et al. (2009: 14), in *Research Methods for Social Workers*, argue: "Knowledge derived from research, although certainly imperfect and still subject to unethical distortions, is the knowledge most likely to help us do our jobs as social workers effectively. It relies on the use of the scientific method." The authors add that certain characteristics of the scientific method set it apart from other sources of knowledge: science is empirical, strives for objectivity and employs specific rules, procedures and techniques. Allen Rubin and Earl Babbie (2008: 20) in their text *Research Methods for Social Work* state: "When we use the scientific method, we should search for evidence that is based on observation as the basis of knowledge.... Scientific observations should be systematic, comprehensive, and as objective as possible." The new paradigm, however, challenges this view, arguing that science and research are not and should not be neutral. As social work researchers and as social workers, we need to critically examine our own beliefs when conducting research. Do we agree that the positivist scientific method is the most legitimate approach to acquiring knowledge, or are we in favour of other methods? To help us get in touch with our deeply held beliefs about research, we need to engage in reflexive exercises. But first let's examine more carefully the nature of paradigms.

Paradigms

Paradigms are systems of knowledge that guide how we think and act. Thomas Kuhn, in his landmark book *The Structure of Scientific Revolutions*, describes paradigms as "universally recognized scientific achievements that for a time provide model problems and solutions to a community of practitioners" 1970: viii). Yvonna Lincoln and Egon Guba (1985), in their text entitled *Naturalistic Inquiry*, explain that paradigms are a distillation of what we think. Paradigms provide us with a framework for making sense of our world. For instance, within the structural social work paradigm, we take it for granted that clients should not be blamed for their socio-economic situation. However, paradigms can be constraining:

> A paradigm is a worldview, a general perspective, a way of breaking down the complexity of the real world. As such, paradigms are deeply imbedded in the socialization of adherents and practitioners: paradigms tell them what is important, legitimate, and reasonable. Paradigms are also normative, telling the practitioner what to do without the necessity of long existential or epistemological consideration. But it is this aspect that constitutes both their strength and their weakness — their strength in that it makes action possible, their weakness in that the very reason for action is hidden in the unquestioned assumptions of the paradigm. (Patton 1978, cited in Lincoln and Guba 1985: 15)

Most of us are not conscious of the paradigm we follow as we plan our actions. As Michael Patton states, paradigms provide unquestioned assumptions about our world and how we should function within it. Such assumptions are situated in our cultural, social and historical context.

Paradigm Shifts

Kuhn (1970) states that paradigm shifts do not occur in an orderly, evolutionary manner. Rather, they are the result of dramatic revolutions, and each subsequent paradigm competes with its predecessors in its claim to provide the most complete explanation of the order of things. In the West, we have gone through significant paradigm shifts. Lincoln and Guba (1985) identify three major paradigms in terms of scientific knowledge: pre-positivism, positivism (or modernism) and post-positivism (interpretivism).

Pre-Positivism

The pre-positivist era, or what many historians have labelled the pre-Enlightenment era (Kuhn 1970), stretched roughly from the time of the ancient Greek philosophers, 450 Before Common Era (BCE), to the time of the British empiricists, 1800 Common Era (CE) (Lincoln and Guba 1985). This period began with the Roman Empire and ended with the Renaissance. The Roman Catholic Church was the chief source of knowledge for most of this time, and the most influential philosopher was Aristotle. Pre-positivism

11

was marked by passive observation of natural phenomena; humans were not trying to control nature but simply wanted to understand its laws.

Positivism

The positivist era, also called the modernist era, began in Europe roughly at the start of the Industrial Revolution. The movement started slowly and gained momentum during the early part of the nineteenth century. New technologies were invented which facilitated the rapid spread of industrialization (Lincoln and Guba 1985).

The term "positivism" was coined by nineteenth-century French sociologist Auguste Comte (Neuman and Kreuger 2003). The most influential advocates were a group of philosophers collectively known as the Vienna Circle of Logical Positivists (Lincoln and Guba 1985: 19). Their approach to research "amounted to the methodological assertion that any variable which cannot be directly represented by a measurement operation has no place in science" (Ford 1975, cited in Lincoln and Guba 1985: 45). This operation of measurement is the kind of active intervention that sets positivism apart from passive observation.

However, it was not just in philosophy that the positivist movement was influential. Positivists had (and still have) an extremely optimistic evaluation of the potential of science. They believe that science will allow humankind to conquer famine and disease and generally lead us toward a better world. Positivism led to the adoption of the scientific method as the dominant set of techniques to understand ourselves and our world.

It was also during the positivist/modernist era that social work developed. As Malcolm Payne (2005) explains, social work is a product of modernism, even though a range of perspectives operate within it. The role of social work within the modernist paradigm is to ensure that people function within societal norms. The assumption of a modernist perspective is similar to that of the order perspective, described in Chapter One: society is functioning in an orderly fashion and social problems result from people not respecting the rules. As such, Payne believes that one of the original purposes of social work was to maintain the social order and enforce the status quo. In agreeing with this point of view, Merlinda Weinberg (2010: 40) suggests that self reflection needs to occur within the profession regarding the benefits to social work professionals in keeping the "poor poor and the marginalized marginalized."

Regarding research specifically, positivism, as Christina Marlow (2005) explicates in *Research for Generalist Social Work*, is linked to empiricist principles, which hold that only knowledge based on direct observation through the senses can be accepted as scientific fact. Empiricist principles include the following:

1. *Objectivity*: To the greatest extent possible, the researcher's values should not interfere with the study of the problem. This means that things that are being observed must not be affected in any way by the person doing the observing or measuring. Positivism would claim that a gay or lesbian person could not do research on sexuality, as their personal sexual preferences would get in the way of their objectivity. (Curiously, the same positivists would likely not see a heterosexual man doing the same kind of research as compromising objectivity.)

2. *Causality*: The positivist strives to find cause-and-effect relationships. Causality means that a change in one factor (x) produces changes in another factor (y). For example, an evaluation of an anger management program might hope to demonstrate that the program causes service users to exhibit fewer hostile outbursts. To establish causality, the following three conditions must be met: 1) a statistical association has to exist; 2) factor x must occur before factor y; and 3) the relationship between factors x and y must be logically linked.

3. *Deductive Reasoning*: Positivism is based largely on deductive reasoning, which means moving from the general to the specific. For example, the general principle is that racism continues to be widespread in our society. Therefore, in applying this principle, a specific person of colour will likely have experienced racism.

4. *Quantitative Methods*: Positivism relies on quantitative methods, where the categories are determined prior to the study and assigned numerical values. Studies are conducted using a standardized measurement instrument with closed-ended, as opposed to open-ended, questions, which provides a numerical score. An example of a quantitative, closed-ended question is: "On a scale of 1 to 5, with 1 being strongly disagree to 5 being strongly agree, 'Do you think the police department is doing a good job?'" An example of an open-ended question is: "What does it mean to you to say that police should be involved in the community?"

5. *Generalizations*: The results must be generalizable to a large group. For example, the results of a pilot study evaluating the effectiveness of a new intervention approach, conducted with a group of inner-city residents in Winnipeg, should be applicable to similar service users all over Canada or North America.

These empiricist principles have had and continue to have a profound influence on the way we think. Most western social workers accept the scientific method as the most legitimate way to achieve knowledge. In their struggle to prove the effectiveness of social work practice, for example, most traditional social work researchers turn to the scientific method, with its controlled "objective" experimentation and a "causal" explanation (Payne 2005).

Post-Postitivism

The beginning of post-postitivism (also called post-modernism or interpretation) is unclear as much of the western world is still largely in the grip of positivism. Nevertheless, particularly in the social sciences, including social work, the assumptions of positivism are being challenged. While some positivists insist that all knowledge is a kind of interpretation, believing that these interpretations can be shared and verified by all people, interpretivists emphasize that the values of the researcher cannot be separated from the research; in other words, objectivity is not possible, nor is it desirable. While positivists believe that the researcher observes phenomena from an external vantage point, the post-positivist believes that the researcher and the phenomenon are enmeshed. All of us observe the world through our own individual lenses, which have been shaped by our cultural values and traditions. This "interpretism" proposes that reality depends to some degree on people's definition of it (Marlow 2005). Interpretist principles include the following:

1. *Subjectivity*: The interpretive researcher is interested in people's definition of reality, in other words, in the meaning they ascribe to reality. This is in recognition that there is not just one reality, and everyone's reality is different.
2. *Description*: Interpretist researchers are interested in understanding as opposed to establishing causality. For example, in what is called formative evaluation, the interpretist researcher looks at the effectiveness of a program from the perspective of staff and service users using open-ended interviews and questionnaires. In contrast, the positivist researcher would conduct what is called a summative evaluation, which seeks to establish a causal relationship between the program and changes in the service users.
3. *Inductive Reasoning*: Interpretism is based largely on inductive reasoning, which means moving from the specific to the general. Interpretist researchers recognize that everyone experiences reality differently, and therefore it does not make sense to apply a general rule to individual cases.
4. *Qualitative Methods*: Qualitative methods involve using words rather than numbers. The interpretist researcher is interested in people's stories and not in gathering numbers.

Positivism and Social Work

In 1892, sociology began to gain hold as a legitimate discipline. At the University of Chicago, white male sociologists carried out research while female sociologists carried out applied sociology in settlement houses, such as Hull House. This gendered context led to the division of social work and sociology in North America. The women of Hull House (the most famous of whom was Jane Addams) formed the foundation of social work knowledge, but their impact was not limited to social work. Their 1895 publication *Hull-House Maps and Papers*, which analyzed the "effects of social disorganization, immigration, and the economy on the everyday life of an urban neighbourhood," established the "substantive interests and methodological technique of Chicago Sociology" (Deegan 1988: 24). Thus, the relationship between social work and sociological knowledge has always been marked by interdependence.

By 1917, the profession of social work separated more decisively from sociology as Mary Richmond published *Social Diagnosis*, the first comprehensive social work text. These two publications are emblematic of the early transition in social work knowledge from research rooted in the ideals of social reform to "scientific" or apolitical research (Deegan 1988). The transition towards the scientific method was seen as critical for the legitimatization of social work as a profession (Margolin 1997).

W. Lawrence Neuman (2006) regards the growth of positivist research methods in social work and the social sciences generally as directly related to pressure from private foundations and other funding bodies, university administrators who wanted to avoid unconventional politics, a desire by researchers for prestige, status and a public image of serious professionalism and the information needs of expanding government and corporate bureaucracies. This push for "objective," value-free research displaced locally based studies that were largely action-oriented, qualitative and run by social reformers, who were often women. As discussed in Kirby, Greaves and Reid (2006b), positivist research generally reflects the voice of privileged social groups. For credible positivist research, researchers must be well schooled in the scientific method and have access to resources that enable them to conduct the research. Research produced by those of a privileged position in society will likely reflect the views and biases of the privileged. Such research effectively silences the voices of those who do not have access to these resources.

Interestingly, even some positivists argue that scientific knowledge is not a sufficient approach to social work. These writers assert that "artistic knowledge" more effectively captures the intuitive, subjective, passionate and creative aspects of social work knowledge (England 1986; Transken 2002; Leavy 2009). For these authors, key aspects of social work knowledge are not represented or understood though science. One example of this is a study involving refugee children that used photographs, a hope quilt and the development of narratives that allowed the children to share their experiences with their parents and other adults (Yohani 2008). There remains, to this day, much debate and tension between those who believe in the dominant paradigm of science as the legitimate base of social work knowledge and those who argue that social work knowledge is more eclectic.

Post-positivist writers argue that science subjugates knowledge and that new approaches to social work knowledge need to "install the client as an important site of knowledge" (Rossiter 2000: 27). Interpretivist researchers see the scientific method as limiting the multiple voices that can contribute to the construction of social work knowledge, arguing that the rigour and rigidity of experimental methods cannot account for the "complexity of human relations and interventions" (Trinder 2000: 42). Carrie Hammers and Allan Brown (2004: 86) argue that positivist approaches to research are inconsistent within a queer context: "Traditional, distinctly modern social scientific approaches that adhere to objectivity, detachment and clear demarcations of the boundaries between researcher-researched, are inadequate to explore identity formations." Hence interpretive methods rebalance empiricist methods "with subjective, intuitive and inductive approaches, thus lending support to new paradigms which integrate theorizing, practice and research as part of holistic experience" (Fook 1996: 197).

Marxist and Feminist Research Paradigms

As stated in Chapter One, structural social work is based on Marxist and feminist theories. An extensive literature demonstrates that Marxism has had a profound impact on social work (Mullaly 2007; Payne 2005; Lundy 2004). For instance, the Marxist dialectic method of analysis has received a lot of attention in social work literature, particularly within the structural social work perspective (Moreau 1979; Mullaly 2007). As Bob Mullaly explains, the dialectic method sensitizes social workers to the opposing and contradictory forces within capitalism and "helps social work to avoid the construction of false dichotomies or dualisms that have been part of the social work tradition" (Mullaly 2007: 237). In other words, using the dialectical method would allow the social worker to understand that the social welfare state has positive elements, in that it provides people with a minimum standard of living, and that investment in the welfare state could potentially lead to a more equitable society. They would also see the negative side of social welfare, in that it can be used as an instrument of social control. An example of this is workfare, which requires people to work as a condition of receiving welfare benefits. In the same vein, social work agencies may house both positive humanistic and negative coercive elements. The dialectic method provides social workers (and their clients) with a tool to understand these contradictions.

Marxism also provides social work with different perspectives on the role of social welfare in society. Marxists are generally critical of the welfare state, suggesting that it is an instrument used by the capitalist to 1) reduce working-class antagonism to the existing social order; 2) increase the efficiency of the economic system; and 3) underwrite the costs that the owners of capital incur (Mullaly 2007: 149). In this sense, capitalists use welfare to avert social disruption. Bismark, who was nicknamed the "Iron Chancellor," developed social welfare in Germany during the later part of the nineteenth century, not out of a concern for humanity but as an instrument of social control, particularly to stop the rising popularity of the socialist movement (Mullaly 2007).

Building on Marxism, feminist theory focuses on the effects of patriarchy to explain the structural inequality of men and women. Since traditional paradigms were all constructed by men, the feminist paradigm is offered as an alternative to these traditional paradigms, which are "gender blind" (Mullaly 2007: 161). There are different forms of feminism, and while all deal with inequality, they vary on the explanations and solutions. For instance, liberal feminism seeks to promote equal opportunities through legislation. Radical feminism focuses on men's power and privilege and seeks to promote separate women's structures. Marxist feminism targets structured inequality in a class-based system. More recently, post-modern feminism has been deconstructing conventional explanations to create an opening for a diverse range of explanations and behaviour (Payne 2005).

With respect to research, there are two feminist epistemologies, feminist empiricism and feminist standpoint. Accepting that the norms of scientific research are sound, feminist empiricists believe that the basic principles of empiricism should not be rejected. However, they assert that traditional empiricism can be "improved" by making certain modifications, because science is not value-free and the scientific method is not sufficient to screen out the influence of these values. While acknowledging that values permeate scientific inquiry, they do not regard values as undermining science because values themselves can be evaluated (Tanesini 1999).

Feminist standpoint, on the other hand, acknowledges the role of the researcher as an active participant in the research and focuses on the experience of women in a patriarchal world. While there are a number of different definitions of feminist standpoint, the one chosen for this chapter comes from one of the original contributors of standpoint theory, Nancy Hartsock. She proposes using Marxist theory as a methodological base to develop an epistemological tool, feminist standpoint, for understanding and opposing class domination:

> I will suggest that, like the lives of the proletariat according to Marxian Theory, women's lives make available a particular and privileged vantage point on male supremacy, a vantage point which can ground a powerful critique of the phallocratic institutions and ideology which constitute the capitalist from of patriarch. (1983: 284)

Marxists believe that only people who have been oppressed by a system can fully understand how that system functions (Payne 2005). Therefore, workers have a privileged perspective to understand the oppression created by the capitalist system, and women have a privileged perspective to understand the oppression created by patriarchy.

As stated in Chapter One, approaches based on Marxism, feminism and structuralism are all part of an umbrella term for social justice oriented approaches to social work. Social work is committed to social justice and social change, and the aim of social work research should be the same. For example, by conducting research that reveals the impact of government cuts, we may be able to show policy-makers that investing in social programs makes good economic sense.

Reflexivity

As stated in the beginning of this chapter, social work researchers need to be aware of the research paradigm that frames our thinking. This can be achieved by engaging in reflexive exercises. Susan Strega (2007: 77) defines reflexivity as "continually thinking about... our values, beliefs, and social location" (also see Payne 2005). Jan Fook (1996) explores the elements of reflexivity, or critical reflection and practice, which include reflection as a process (cognitive, emotional, experiential) of examining assumptions embedded in actions or experience; a linking of these assumptions with many different origins (personal, emotional, social, cultural, historical, political); and a review and re-evaluation of these according to relevant criteria. A quote from a student's reflexive journal illustrates Fook's thoughts:

> A final point that I would like to address in this reflexive journal is on the topic of bias. I acknowledge the importance of revisiting my own biases throughout this research process. This fits into the post-positivist paradigm which acknowledges that there is no such thing as an objective or value-free researcher. I identify as straight. I am researching a community to whom I do not consider myself a member. Perhaps more than the other members of my group, I need to be conscious and reflective of... Straight Mind... wherein all of history, culture, social reality, language and all subjective phenomena are interpreted and understood via a heterosexual lens.[1]

Social work researchers should use reflexivity to examine our beliefs about the scientific method. To reiterate the question posed at the beginning of this chapter: do our beliefs fit within the positivist paradigm, or are we genuinely open to other methods of acquiring knowledge? Put another way, are we stuck in the positivist paradigm without being aware of it, leaving us closed to what our participants may be requesting? Literature related to action research discusses the importance of reflexivity as part of the process (Etmanski and Pant 2007).

Colin Stuart and Bessa Whitmore (2006), who taught the research course to MSW students at Carleton University, used reflexive exercises to help students get in touch with their beliefs. They point out that, in the process of conducting research and reflecting upon the experience, students find meaningful connections to practice. Their students reported that, as a result of their reflexive exercises, research was demystified and was seen as a practical skill that could be integrated into their practice skills.

John Peters and Annie Gray (2007: 321) describe how they incorporate reflection as an integral component of their Action Research course. They do so purposively as a way of pushing their students to examine the assumptions and framework that guides their practice and thinking:

> This is a model that describes a cyclical process of reflection and action culminating in a systemic inquiry into one's practice and practical theories. Participants learn about each step and what is required from them as they take each step. They prepare a written description of each step, one at a time, and they submit their written work to all other participants for critique and feedback. Participants give their oral feedback in class and written responses online in the form of posts on Blackboard, the web based course management system. Each participant also posts his or her reflections on the week's class based experience. These reflections serve as the basis for further discussion and dialogue about the teaching and learning process, readings, the research process, and other aspects of the course experience.

We close this chapter on paradigms with a quote from a student describing his thoughts about a debate he had with some of his fellow students:

> When presenting our ethics proposal to the class, I had the frustrating experience of presenting a methodology I felt reasonably confident with, and which seemed to me to be transparent, only to find that this view was not shared by others. Instead, we experienced much resistance to the quantitative nature of our research design. I admit, I was a bit defensive in my response to our critics. However, Smith suggests that "a helpful response to this is not to retreat to the ivory tower cursing the scientific illiteracy or innumeracy of social workers, but to recognize that change is difficult and can be threatening and always takes time" (1987: 412). Our class discussion led into a more global discussion of research methodology in social work. Specifically, some members of the class displayed much disagreement regarding the application of positivist research paradigm within social

work. This class debate was a nice reflection of the debate that continues within the field of social work (e.g., the Sheldon-Jordon debate, cited in Smith, 1987: 403).[2]

DISCUSSION QUESTIONS

1. Is it possible to acknowledge that values are part of research but still be objective?
2. Are all observations coloured by perception, values and assumptions?
3. What do you think science is?
4. Do you have previous experience engaging in research? If so, how does this influence your opinion on the paradigm in which you were trained?
5. Which of the positivist and interpretivist paradigms best represents your concept of science?
6. How might you envision using a structural approach to research?
7. What challenges do you see in using the structural approach in your research?

Notes

1. Catherine Brohman, Reflexive Journal, 2010.
2. Charles Furlotte, Reflexive Journal, November 2007.

3. Research Ethics

Any organization, such as a university, hospital, school board, government institution and social service agency, conducting research involving people (formally called human subjects, now called research participants) must undergo an ethical review process. With the passing of the *National Research Act* in 1974, this became a legal requirement in the United States. While not yet a legal obligation in Canada, larger organizations such as hospitals, school boards and universities have research ethics boards (REBs). In addition, social workers have a professional obligation to protect the interests of research participants, and to this end the Canadian Association of Social Workers (CASW) has established ethical principles concerning research. For instance, Value Statement 6 states: "Social workers who engage in research minimize risks to participants, ensure informed consent, maintain confidentiality and accurately report the results of their studies" (CASW 2005). The U.S. National Association of Social Workers (NASW) has also adopted ethical principles concerning research.

These measures are an improvement over past practices, when the interests of "science" took precedence over the needs of the individual participants. One infamous example of this is the Milgram (1983) study of obedience to authority. Milgram, a psychologist with Stanford University, wanted to test how far people would acquiesce to authority over the dictates of their conscience. In his experiment, so-called "teachers" (who were the subjects of the experiment but did not know this) were asked to administer an electrical shock of increasing intensity to a "learner" for each mistake they made during the experiment. The fictitious story given to these "teachers" was that the experiment was exploring effects of punishment for incorrect responses on learning behaviour. The "teacher" was not aware that the "learner" was an actor faking discomfort as the "teacher" increased the intensity of the electric shocks. In reality, no one was being shocked — a tape recorder with pre-recorded screams was hooked up to play each time the teacher administered a shock. The "learner's" behaviour escalated with each fake shock from banging on the walls, to begging the teacher to stop, to dead silence. "Teachers" tended to become distressed and would ask to stop the experiment, at which time they were told to please continue, that the experiment required that they continue, that it was absolutely essential that they continue. If the "teacher" still asked to stop the experiment, it was terminated. Only fourteen out of forty "teachers" halted the experiment before administering a 450 volt shock, though every participant questioned the experiment and no "teacher" firmly refused to stop the shocks before 300 volts. Many of the research participants, the "teachers," experienced psychological problems after the experiment. The research participants were deceived about the true nature of the study and they did not give consent to and were not protected from participating in a study that caused them harm.

What Is Ethics?

The word ethics comes from the Greek word *ethos*, which refers to a moral custom and is used to identify a set of principles around what is right or wrong. When applied to research, ethical issues are the "concerns, dilemma and conflicts that arise over the proper way to conduct research" (Neuman and Kreuger 2003: 98). Ethical principles are the rules or guidelines to be followed by the researcher to ensure that the interests of the human participants are protected. These principles as they apply to social work are included in the NASW or CASW codes of ethics.

History of Ethical Considerations in Research

As stated earlier, the belief that there are ethical considerations in research, let alone the need for an ethics review, is relatively recent. Before the last few decades, the interests of science were considered more important than those of individual participants. The need for research ethics was made clear by dramatic events in our history showing what can happen when science takes precedence. People, or "subjects" as they would have been thought of then, were exposed to the most brutal treatments in the name of science. An extreme but nevertheless real example was the case of unethical medical experiments carried out by Nazi physicians on concentration camp prisoners. In order to study bone and nerve regeneration, Nazi doctors carried out bone and nerve transplants on unwilling participants without anesthesia. This case led to the adoption of the Nuremberg Code in 1947, which states that subjects must voluntarily consent to participate in research (Berg 2007).

Another example, closer to home, was the Tuskegee Syphilis Study. The purpose of this study, which began in 1932 and continued until the early 1970s, was to identify the consequences of untreated syphilis on a population of poor African American men. While the men were not deliberately infected, they were promised free treatment for "bad blood" when in fact they were deprived (without their consent) of treatment with penicillin, which was discovered in the 1930s (Berg 2007). A U.S. Senate inquiry into this case was convened in 1972, when Jean Heller, an Associated Press reporter, broke the story and was instrumental in the passing of the *National Research Act*, mentioned above.

Canada also had its share of examples. For instance, testimony given at the Truth Commission into Genocide in Canada revealed that, in the early part of the twentieth century, under the guise of medical research, Aboriginal children in the Nanaimo Tuberculosis Hospital (then called the "Indian Hospital") were subjected to medical experiments and deliberately infected with tuberculosis (Annett 2001). During the 1960s, CIA-funded experiments were conducted at the Allen Memorial Hospital in Montreal on the effects of LSD on psychiatrically hospitalized individuals (Dyck 2005). These events dramatically highlighted the need for considering the ethics of research prior to undertaking any study.

While these examples are dramatic, it is still necessary to consider how to protect participants from more subtle harm. For example, when doing program evaluation, it is important that the service users feel that they can refuse to participate and not be denied services in the future and that staff members who provided the services are not present when the clients are being interviewed.

The principles of research ethics are constantly evolving, and REBs need to keep up with changes. Nevertheless, the overarching purpose of REBs is to ensure that the interests of science do not take precedence over protection of participants from undue risk and that participants provide free and informed consent. However, we believe that social work research needs to go beyond simply protecting participants. Social workers should adhere to a structural approach and the principles of anti-oppressive practice. While mainstream social workers consider the researcher to be neutral and objective, structural AOP social workers understand that social work research is not a neutral political process. It therefore requires research to be shared between researchers and participants. Social work researchers are encouraged to think about the impact of the results on their clients and to use the results in a manner consistent with the structural approach, i.e., as an impetus to social change. Thus, self-reflection and ongoing social analysis, in addition to sound research methodology, are essential components of social justice oriented social work practice.

Much of this approach to social work research, and the structural approach itself, can be traced back to the influence of feminist social work practice and research. Feminist research acknowledges the role of women participants as active partners in the research and focuses on the experience of women in a patriarchal world (Tanesini 1999). While mainstream social work would prefer to remain politically neutral or non-partisan, feminist researchers take an overtly political position against patriarchy (Harding

1987) and also validate the unique experience of women as experts on their lives (Smith 1987).

Tri-Council Policy Statement

For university-based research, we have the Tri-Council Policy Statement on Ethical Conduct for Research Involving Humans (2005). The Tri Council encompasses three organizations, the Canadian Institute of Health Research (CIHR), the Natural Sciences and Engineering Research Council of Canada (NSERC) and the Social Sciences and Humanities Research Council of Canada (SSHRC), which are the primary federal government agencies that fund research in Canada. The mandate of the Tri-Council is to promote research that is conducted according to the highest ethical standards and to ensure that researchers and their institutions apply the ethical principles. According to the Tri-Council Statement, research ethics should include: "(1) the selection and achievement of morally acceptable ends and, (2) the morally acceptable means to those ends" (2005, section B i.4). With respect to the latter, the Tri-Council makes clear that it does not support tricking a person into participating by means of promising false benefits, such as suggesting overly optimistic intervention outcomes. The specific policies are based on the following eight guiding principles, which the Tri-Council believes respect the standards, values and aspirations of the research community (section C, i.4-5):

1. *Respect for Human Dignity*: The Tri-Council strives to protect the multiple and interdependent interests of the person from bodily or psychological harm and to respect cultural integrity.
2. *Respect for Free and Informed Consent*: Individuals have the capacity and the right to make informed decisions. This means that they must be fully informed about real or possible risks as well as any benefits, direct or indirect.
3. *Respect for Vulnerable Persons*: Individuals, such as children, institutionalized persons or persons with disabilities, who may have diminished competence in terms of their ability to understand the risks and benefits associated with their participation require special procedures to ensure their protection. Vulnerable persons are a majority of the people that social workers engage with in research.
4. *Respect for Privacy and Confidentiality*: Respect for human dignity includes the right to privacy and confidentiality in terms of control, access and dissemination of personal information.
5. *Respect for Justice and Inclusiveness*: Individuals have a fundamental right to be treated with fairness and equity. Populations who have been traditionally mistreated or who are otherwise vulnerable by virtue of race, class,

gender, sexual orientation or disability may require special consideration to ensure their protection.

6. *Balancing Harms and Benefits*: REBs regularly have to choose between harms and benefits. The basic principle is that the harms should not outweigh the benefits. These decisions are particularly challenging with research that is innovative and involves the advancement of frontiers of knowledge.

7. *Minimizing Harm*: Related to the above is the importance of ensuring that individuals are not exposed to unnecessary risks. This means that if the research necessarily involves human subjects, the number of subjects and tests must be kept to a minimum.

8. *Maximizing Benefits*: Researchers have a duty to ensure that their work results in benefits to human kind. This is particularly true for professions like social work, which has an obligation to carry out research directly relevant to practice.

Appendix 1 is a letter advertising an upcoming research project which illustrates how these eight principles are put into practice.

Research Ethics Boards and Institutional Review Boards

In Canada, the Tri-Council Policy Statement specifies the membership of research ethics boards, which must be made up of at least five members, including both men and women. The Tri-Council specifies that at least two members have "broad expertise in the methods or in the areas of research that are covered by the REB" (article 1.3). It also requires that at least one member has no affiliation with the institution but is recruited from the community that is served by the institution. The role of the REB is "to approve, reject, propose modifications to or terminate any proposed or ongoing research involving human subjects that is conducted with, or by members of, the institution" (article 1.2). The Tri-Council Policy Statement adds that the REB must have the appropriate financial and administrative independence to fulfill their duties. The institution may not override a negative decision without a formal appeal process.

In the United States, federal regulations require that institutional review boards (IRB) be made up of at least five members from varying backgrounds to ensure an adequate and complete review. The regulations also state that the membership should not be made up of exclusively men, women or a single racial group or profession, nor should it be made up of only social scientists but should include professionals from other fields such as law or medicine. Given these regulations, it is conceivable that no one on the IRB has any research experience. This poses significant challenges for researchers in that these members may not appreciate the importance of scientific rigour.

In fact, researchers have complained that IRBs have become too restrictive, stating that IRBs have become "handcuffs impeding their search for scientific answers to social problems" (Berg 2007: 61). Berg suggests that finding a balance between ensuring the safety of human subjects and supporting unhampered research is no easy task.

One example of the restrictiveness of REBs and IRBs is that they do not always understand the purpose and important contribution that can be made by an advisory board. They often consider members of an advisory board to be potential participants, who therefore cannot be consulted about the research until the project has passed through the ethics review process. One of our students discusses her frustration with this in her research journal:

> In an ideal world, I would have chosen to consult some community members not connected with (the agency as part of an advisory committee in order to ensure that their instrument was inclusive and contained all of the questions needed to answer their research question), in order to increase the level of social action and potential for social change. Of course, practically speaking, we could not begin interviewing community members before receiving ethics clearance, and we could not receive ethics clearance until we had already completed our survey questions. We could not go out in the community to invite parents to come and sit on the advisory committee at such an early stage in the research process.[1]

Ethical Issues

According to the Tri-Council Statement, there are a number of ethical issues to be addressed in any ethics review application. The following seven issues are salient for a structural perspective and AOP principles:

1. *Informed Consent*: The first and arguably most important issue is that participants must be fully aware of what the research is about and what is being asked of them. Participants must clearly understand the risks and benefits. While not all research requires written permission, as a general rule, the greater the risk of potential harm, the greater the need for the researcher to obtain written consent (Neuman and Kreuger 2003). Here again, we believe that participants should not only be fully informed of the purpose of the research and the risks and benefits, but they should also be fully involved.

   There are two types of consent: active and passive. Active consent is defined as formal consent by a participant agreeing to participate. In the case of children (under sixteen in most jurisdictions), a parent or guardian must sign the consent form. Passive consent is where the participant is deemed to provide consent simply by participating in the research. For instance, it would be illogical to obtain written consent from a participant for completing an anonymous (on-line, mailed-out) questionnaire. In this case, information about the purpose of the research, as well as potential risks and benefits involved must be sent along with the questionnaires. Online surveys often include a short description of the research as well as the benefits and risks, and participants must acknowledge that they have read this description before they can continue to answer the survey. This applies to mailed surveys as well, as there would often be no direct face-to-face contact between the participant and the researcher. Depending on the nature of the questions, most of these surveys would involve little if any risk to the participant.

Notwithstanding the importance of voluntary participation, there is a debate among researchers about the drawbacks to active informed consent. Some researchers claim that asking for written consent discourages participation (Berg 2007). If there is a poor response rate, the integrity of the research and the generalizability of the results may be called into question. Others argue that the risk in foregoing active informed consent is that participants are less likely to be fully aware of the nature of the research. This is a slippery slope and may bring us back to the days when the interest of advancing scientific knowledge took precedence.

For research conducted within Aboriginal communities, the debate includes whether the community or the REB (or both) needs to grant informed consent beforehand. Aboriginal communities have had a long history of research being done *on* them. Increasingly, these communities are insisting on more control in the design of the research, how the data will be used and how the results will be interpreted or disseminated (Brascoupé and Mann 2001). Appendix 2 provides an example of a typical consent form.

2. *Risks*: Of great concern to REBs is the real or potential risk to the participants. The general rule is that the greater the risk, the greater the scrutiny required by the REB. Much of the research carried out in social work involves some psychological or emotional risk. For example, by asking participants to re-live painful experiences, the researcher may inadvertently provoke a strong emotional reaction, which may require the help of a trained professional. Researchers studying the pre- and post-migration trauma experienced by Iraqi immigrants explored how to help these immigrants cope with the depression that was caused by this trauma. They informed participants that re-telling their stories could cause emotional distress and that they would be provided with help if necessary (Jamil, Nassar and Lambert 2007). In cases like this, arrangements need to be made ahead of time to ensure that a professional counsellor is available if needed.

3. *Benefits*: Most social work research will not result in immediate benefits to the participants. For instance, program evaluations or needs assessments may provide information to help future or potential clients but not necessarily the clients participating in the study. One example of this was a resource centre which asked community members what gaps existed in the services they provided. They discovered that the centre was not providing services relevant to the growing Asian community. The resource centre director stated: "The Chinese community wasn't even on our radar" (Schwartz 2010). While the participants of the study may not have benefitted, they helped future members because the centre hired a worker who spoke Mandarin and began a group for new Chinese immigrants. More and more researchers are providing a small sum of money as an honorarium to participants in recognition that their time is valuable.

4. *Confidentiality*: Confidentiality is one of the cornerstones of ethical research. Confidentiality means that the information provided by the participant will be used anonymously. Participants have the right to have their privacy protected. This applies to their personal information and the views expressed during interviews. Researchers need to state that they will only report data that cannot be attributed to any specific individual, or if the individual can be identified, the information can only be used with the participant's permission.

In some research situations, ensuring confidentiality is impossible, for instance, in the case of focus groups, where several participants are interviewed together. The researcher cannot control what information participants share and to whom outside of the focus group.

Research involving a participatory action research (PAR) approach can be even more problematic. If community members are involved in data gathering and analysis, they may not appreciate the importance of respecting each individual's need for confidentiality. Here again, participants need to be fully informed about these possibilities.

Lastly, researchers and especially social work researchers must inform participants of instances when they have to violate confidentiality. If a participant discusses abuse of a child under the age of sixteen, a social worker has a legal responsibility to report this to child welfare authorities. In Nova Scotia, Ontario and Newfoundland, the law identifies professionals as having the responsibility to report suspected child abuse or neglect. Other provinces, such as Saskatchewan, Prince Edward Island and British Columbia, extend this responsibility to all persons (Regehr and Kanani 2010). While it is rare that a person discloses such abuse, the interviewer must be prepared to deal with this situation. It is important to include in your letter of consent a disclaimer that says that if a participant discusses harm to themselves or others, this information may have to be reported to the authorities. Appendix 2 shows an example of a letter of consent including this disclaimer. If a participant discusses harm to a child you must remind them of the disclaimer in your consent form. It is good practice to ask the participant to make the call to the authorities themselves with you present as a support. However, if they refuse to do so, the worker must end the interview and contact the authorities. Colleen Lundy (2004) gives a good example of how to address this issue. While her example was meant for social work practioners we have changed it slightly to be relevant for research participants as well:

> Normally what you say during this interview is held in confidence. This means that I will not discuss what you say with anyone outside of the research team who are analyzing the data we collect in our research. However, there are some exceptions. If you mention, or I suspect, that you or a family member have abused or neglected a child, I must report this to the Children's Aid Society. If possible, I would assist you in making the report yourself. If you say anything about causing harm to yourself or others, I have the responsibility of notifying the person at risk or other appropriate authorities.

5. *Anonymity*: Anonymity is closely linked to confidentiality and involves not identifying which participants were included in the study. Anonymity disallows the identification of participants by name, organization, position or any other identifying factors. Anonymity may become an issue when an organization has an interest in knowing who participated. In the case of program evaluations, clients may not want to be seen going into an interview with the researcher. Anonymity, however, is often difficult to guarantee because some outside person may observe a participant attending an interview and report back to the organization. Researchers have to be very clear about whether they can guarantee the anonymity of the participant.

6. *Data Storage and Access*: Part of protecting the privacy and confidentiality of participants involves keeping the raw data in a secure location. Transcripts or completed questionnaires may contain sensitive information. This data should be kept in a locked filling cabinet. If the data is in an electronic file, access should be password protected. The policy in our university is that the data can only be kept on a computer not connected to the internet. If the computer is connected to the internet, data must be stored on a removable source such as an external hard drive or memory stick, and that equipment must be kept in a locked filing cabinet. Researchers need to state how and where the data will be kept and who will have access.

7. *Destruction of Data*: In most cases, once the study is complete and the final report has been written and disseminated, there is no need to retain the raw data. Paper copies should be shredded, and electronic files, including recordings, videos and photographs, deleted. If the researcher wishes to keep the raw data for some future follow-up research, the participants need to know this ahead of time.

University-based research in Canada must go through a lengthy and thorough ethics application. Such procedures, while not without their problems, at least force researchers to think about the above issues before they go into a community. These ethics reviews ask a raft of questions about matters such as the community to be involved, the nature of their involvement (how participants are recruited, for example), possible conflict of interest on the part of researchers, the potential risks and benefits to the participants and how they are communicated to participants, and the kind of methodology being used and so on. A typical ethics application is included as Appendix 3.

Participatory Action Research and Ethics

We believe that wherever possible, organizations requesting research from social workers or social work students should agree to a participatory action research (PAR) approach. PAR emphasizes empowering communities through actively involving the people affected by the research in all phases of the research (Marlow 2005). PAR is compatible with structural social work principles in that power is shared. Rather than having a principal investigator, control of the research is shared among researchers, participants and others who may be affected by the results of the research, such as community representatives or client associations.

At the same time, PAR poses some difficult challenges for REBs. Most research projects have a designated principal investigator who is ultimately accountable to the REB for the research activity. However, this is difficult to do when power is shared among many people, including researchers and community members. Researchers may not be able to guarantee anonymity or confidentiality, nor will they be able to state how the raw data or the final report will be used. The community may want to make changes to the methodology throughout the research process. In short, a REB faced with a PAR proposal may not know exactly what they are approving or who to hold accountable.

To cite a case example of this challenge, the need to ensure confidentiality was a potential problem in a research project undertaken by some of our graduate social work students. The research described in Chapter One, which involved the identification of community capacities in a low-income housing project, was carried out with the intention of encouraging maximum community participation. The students, who used a structural perspective and were committed to a PAR approach, created a research advisory committee made up of community members whose role it was to help develop the research instrument as well as the methodology. However, the students could not ensure that statements made by research participants would remain confidential if community members were involved in the data collection and analysis. But, in order to maximize the response rate from the community, students felt they had to guarantee confidentiality. As a compromise, students decided against involving community members in the data collection and analysis (Lai, Forster, Head, Helfer and Fuchs 2008).

The only solution for researchers and REBs in this type of situation, and one that is consistent with the principle of "informed consent," is that participants must be fully informed about what it means to participate in a PAR project. If participants understand that fellow community members will be involved in conducting interviews and data analysis, and they still agree to participate, there is no ethical conflict. This may mean that some potential participants will refuse to participate. At the same time, if enough people in the community are committed to the goals of the research, they may be willing to sacrifice their privacy for the sake of helping their community get the information it needs.

The situation is different in the case of grassroots and other small organizations, which will not have an established REB. The following is an example of one community organization's experience with creating their own REB. The research, which was conducted in a low-income community in Ottawa, focused on social inclusion, which involved ensuring that community residents had complete and open access to all programs and services. The steering committee for this project, made up of staff, volunteers and community members, wanted an ethics process that fit their mandate and reflected the values of the community, which were to ensure participatory research methods, equality between researchers and participants, and reflection and action. They strived to achieve balance in the composition of the ethics committee by including at least one male, one long-term resident, a representative ethnic mix, someone who had worked with the community and a community representative with a good knowledge of ethics. The composition of this REB was very different from more traditional REBs such as those belonging to a university. The goals in terms of protecting the interests of the participants were the same, but the means of achieving these goals were different. Unlike traditional REBs, this REB did not maintain an arm's length distance from the project. The REB had members who were both project staff and on the steering committee. As well, representatives of community agencies served on both the REB and the steering committee. Finally, some of the members of the REB also participated in the research in the capacity of community member, staff or community agency representative (Jenkins and Hagi-Aden 2008).

But the strength of this type of REB is also its weakness. While this approach ensures community control in terms of protecting the community and its members, the disadvantage is that members of this REB did not have an arm's length relationship and, in some cases, could have been in a conflict of interest situation.

In spite of ethical challenges discussed above, the benefits of conducting research from a structural perspective using a PAR approach outweigh the challenges. This type of research offers universities important opportunities to leave the "ivory tower" and form partnerships with the community. It also provides communities with a valuable service and students with a chance to engage in practical, hands-on research and to connect with community groups. As universities gain more experience with structurally based research and as communities become better informed about the importance of ethical reviews, solutions will develop, resulting in effective community-based research strategies that protect the participants.

Code of Ethics for Progressive Social Workers

(We believe these capture the ethical principles to be followed in structural social work research.)

- We regard our primary obligation to be the welfare of all humankind across the globe, not just those in our immediate vicinity.
- We understand the contradictions inherent in delivering social services in a capitalist society. We know that the state can be both oppressive and supportive.
- We never claim to be "apolitical" or "neutral" and we define social justice in political, material and global terms, not just in psychological terms.
- We respect the need for resources and decision-making processes to be fairly shared, and we realize that this will be hard to achieve given the current political order.
- We recognize the importance of language and try to show sensitivity through the words that we use. However, we realize that we might "get it wrong."
- We value processes as much as "products" or "outcomes" and we are, at the very least, skeptical of using violence to deal with conflict.
- We define power in possessive and relational ways. This means that while we are wary of calling anyone "powerless," we are also aware of the way dominant groups can exercise power over people who are

oppressed on the basis of race, gender, class, age, sexual orientation, and geographical location.

- Because we strive to live in a society where people are able to exercise their human rights, we try to democratize our professional relationships as well as our personal ones.
- We do not see financial profit as the primary goal in life. Thus, we do not uphold the tenets of global capitalism nor do we value paid work over that which is unpaid.
- While we appreciate the importance of group bonds, we are wary of the way nationalism can be used to deride and exclude others. In so doing, we seek to work with people from diverse backgrounds in equitable and culturally sensitive ways.
- We value education for the ways it can be used to develop critical consciousness.
- We respect the need for oppressed groups to sometimes "go it alone." Yet we do not presume this will always be their preference. Instead, we are open to provide support/resources to oppressed groups in a manner that they suggest will be useful.
- While developing knowledge that will be useful to social transformation, we speak up whenever we can about the acts of unfairness that we see, using all the sorts of media to broadcast our observations and ideas.
- We recognize the potentially conservative nature of all methods of social work, and we strive to radicalize all forms of social work that we undertake. As we do this, we avoid individual acts of heroism or martyrdom, preferring instead to work in collaboration with others.
- We do not see ourselves sitting outside society, or as liberators of the "needy" or the "downtrodden." Rather, we try to use the benefits derived from our professional status to work against the exploitation of individuals and groups.
- We try to do all this in everyday, reflexive ways, without posturing as self-appointed experts.
- Given all the obstacles that confront us, we realize that fatalism, cynicism and despair may set in. To prevent this we try to keep a sense of humour, have fun with other, and incorporate self-care activities into our lives.

Source: Developed by Fraser and Briskman and cited by Bob Mullaly (2007: 54–55).

DISCUSSION QUESTIONS

1. Describe the difference between anonymity and confidentiality.
2. When conducting a focus group, which of the above can you guarantee?
3. What are the similarities and differences between the Code of Ethics for a Progressive Social Worker (see Appendix 1) and the Tri-Council Code?
4. Are there situations where research participants should not be informed about the nature of the study? Explain.

Note

1. Brie Davies, Reflexive Journal entry 2, January 25, 2011.

4. Developing Research Questions

For the most part, social work research follows mainstream research methods and seldom challenges the status quo. Structural social workers, on the other hand, who adhere to anti-oppressive principles, use research as an opportunity to advance social justice and fight against oppressive policies and practices. While the actual research methods used by structural social workers may resemble those of mainstream social work researchers, what sets their work apart is not necessarily the research process but the underlying theoretical perspective. Just as structural social work practice has been influenced by feminist and Marxist theories, so too has structural social work research.

The next few chapters are devoted to the research process, which we describe in a step-by-step, practical manner so that social work students with no background in research will be able to learn the steps without much difficulty. We begin this chapter with what is normally a first step in the research process — the development of the research question or questions. We look at the different types of questions and the criteria used to evaluate good questions, and we provide ideas on sources of questions. Also described are the purpose of and methods for developing the conceptual and theoretical frameworks. This chapter concludes with a description of the literature review, what it is, what role it plays, sources of the literature, how to limit its scope and finally suggestions on writing one.

Research Methods

Before discussing research questions, we should review basic concepts about research. First, as stated earlier, research tends to be organized into two broad methods: quantitative and qualitative. In quantitative research, the data is represented in the form of numbers and the analysis uses descriptive and inferential statistics. In qualitative research, the data is represented primarily in the form of words. The results rely on content analysis to identify themes. In qualitative studies, the ultimate goal is to develop an in-depth understanding of the reality of the people involved in the phenomenon of interest. While quantitative methods have traditionally been associated with positivist principles, qualitative methods follow interpretist principles. Social work research, both mainstream and structural, often relies on both qualitative and quantitative methods. These approaches can complement each other.

The Interpretive (Qualitative) Way of Thinking

As discussed in Chapter Two, quantitative and qualitative methods involve very different paradigms, or ways of thinking. The interpretive way of knowing discards the positivist notion that there is only one external reality. Instead, the interpretive perspective is that reality is defined by the individual participant. Interpretive researchers have been heavily influenced by feminist researchers, who believe that men and women experience the world differently and represent two equally valid realities. As stated by Richard Grinnell, Margaret Williams and Yvonne Unrau (2009), interpretive researchers believe that, in the context of a research interview, there are multiple realities: the researcher's reality; the research participant's reality; and the mutual reality that they create and share.

While positivist researchers believe that values can and should be put aside so that they don't influence the research, interpretive researchers work to develop an awareness of their values and acknowledge the inevitable influence of values. Another difference is that quantitative studies use a deductive process (from the general to the specific), and qualitative studies generally use an inductive process (specific to the general).

The Positivist Way of Knowing

The positivist view is that research must be as "objective" as possible, and it attempts to study only those things that can be "objectively" measured. While physical phenomena are relatively easy to measure, other phenomena, such as values, attitudes and feelings, are not nearly as simple. To a positivist, things that are being observed must not be affected in any way by the person doing the observing or measuring. Positivist researchers will go to great lengths to ensure that their own values or biases do not affect the research results. However, we should stress that complete objectivity is impossible to achieve. As pointed out by Grinnell, Williams and Unrau (2009), it has been discovered that even atoms change by being observed. The positivist-oriented researcher tries to rule out uncertainty. However, since it is impossible to totally rule out uncertainty, conclusions should always be tentative. Positivist researchers try to do research in such a way that the studies can be duplicated, so that other researchers can verify and confirm the results. Finally, positivist researchers put a great deal of emphasis on the use of standardized procedures. In order to establish "scientific" credibility, researchers follow specific steps. The following section outlines those steps.

The Research Question Continuum

Most research questions can be placed along a research continuum, from exploratory at one extreme, through to descriptive and explanatory at the other.

Exploratory Studies

If little is known about a given topic, we would generally engage in an exploratory study. For instance, we may be interested in understanding the problem of bullying in public schools. The research question would be: "What is the nature of bullying in public schools in Ottawa?" In most cases this would involve a qualitative approach, using interviews with key informants, including students, parents, teachers and school administrators.

Descriptive Studies

If we have some knowledge about a topic but we need to know more about the extent of the issue, we would engage in a descriptive study. Using our example of bullying, the question could be: "How extensive is bullying in public schools in Ottawa?" Both quantitative and qualitative approaches would probably be used. This type of question frequently involves a needs assessment (see Chapter Nine) and often relies on a descriptive study such as a large-scale survey.

Explanatory Studies

If we want to know if there is a causal relationship between two phenomena, where one phenomenon, such as an intervention program, would cause a change in another phenomenon, such as the impact on participants, we would adopt an explanatory study. This generally involves a quantitative approach. Again referring to our example on bullying, the research question could be: "How effective are workshops on bullying in terms of reducing the extent of bullying in public schools in Ottawa?" An example of an explanatory study is a summative program evaluation (see Chapter Eight), where we want to know if a certain program will cause an improvement in participants' situations.

Classification of Research Questions

Research questions can be organized according to the nature of the questions. Grinnell, Williams and Unrau (2009) identify the following six types of questions:

1. *Existence Questions*: This type of question is used to determine if a phenomenon actually exists. For instance, if we believe that there is a connection between spousal abuse and self-esteem, the first task is to determine if spousal abuse and self-esteem actually exists in our community. We may assume that spousal abuse and problems with self esteem is an issue in

our community, but without the documented evidence, we are left with our assumptions.

2. *Composition Questions*: This type of question is used to understand more about the phenomenon. We may ask: "What attributes make up self-esteem or spousal abuse?"

3. *Relationship Questions*: Once we understand more about a phenomenon, we may want to know if it is related to other phenomena. The question might be: "Is there a connection between self-esteem and spousal abuse?"

4. *Descriptive-Comparative Questions*: We may want to find out if the phenomenon is experienced differently among different groups. Questions might be: "Does self-esteem differ among heterosexual women versus lesbian women?" "Is self-esteem experienced differently by First Nations women?"

5. *Causality Questions*: We may want to find out if there is a causal relationship among the different phenomena. We would ask: "Does spousal abuse cause women to have low self-esteem?"

6. *Causality-Comparative Questions*: If there is a causal relationship, there may be several factors related to the existence of abuse. We may want to know which factor contributes more to the existence of abuse. We may ask: "Is a person who has been abused more likely to abuse others?" "Is alcohol a factor?"

Formulating Research Questions

It is essential to have a good clear research question in designing an effective study. Here again, Grinnell, Williams and Unrau (2009) identify the following factors that relate to good research questions.

1. *Relevance*: The research question must be relevant to the client, the worker and the organization in question. Studying poverty in Europe is relevant only to the extent that it may provide social policy ideas for Canada. It is important to point out that we should not shy away from research questions that may be "too political." We should remember that our goal is social change, which by its very nature is political. Our research into child poverty has gotten us into political "hot water" on more than one occasion. By documenting the lack of progress in reducing the extent of child poverty, we have put governments at different levels on the defensive for ignoring the problem.

2. *Researchable*: Some questions may be very relevant but are not easily researchable, either because of the nature of the question or the difficulty in getting access to useful data. For instance, some populations, such as homeless youth, are difficult to reach, and any questions concerning this population may be difficult to study. On the other hand, we may

want to consider using non-traditional research strategies for studying these difficult-to-reach populations, who may otherwise be ignored by mainstream researchers. For instance, we could recruit homeless youth as research partners to assist in accessing the data. Some studies may simply not be feasible. It may be a problem getting access to data, or there may simply not be enough resources to fund the study. For instance, getting access to data on sex trade workers or street people is very challenging.

3. *Ethical*: Finally, if there is the potential of harm to the participants or other people who may be affected by the research, it may not be ethical to conduct the research. This is normally determined by a research ethics board. See Chapter Three for a discussion of ethical issues in research.

The organization where the social worker is employed may select the research question, in which case the question is decided for them. The organization may need to study a certain problem. For instance, it may wish to conduct a program evaluation or a client satisfaction survey. Social workers called on to conduct organization-driven research projects may want to recommend having input from clients and community representative by including some of these people on an advisory committee. For a fuller discussion of this see Chapter Five on research partners.

Possible research questions may result from an organization engaging in strategic planning, which is an exercise used to identify goals and objectives as well as program priorities. Quite often the discussion results in questions that need further exploration. For instance, there may be questions about the changing demographics of the client population.

Human Diversity Issues

One issue that is very important is the characteristics of the researcher. In the past, most research was conducted by white, middle-class males. A lot of harm has been done because of gender biased and ethnocentric practices. Structural social work researchers need to be aware of their own biases and how these may influence the choice of research question and design. If the focus of the research is on various ethnic groups, having representatives from the racial and ethnic groups involved will help to minimize further oppression.

Below is an example of a research question formulated by a group of student researchers:

> The goal in conducting this research is to gain more understanding about the capacity of anti-violence programs in the Ottawa area to provide services to LGBTTQ families and individuals who have experienced intimate partner violence or sexual violence. More specifically, this research project aims to assess the com-

fort levels, knowledge, specific needs and gaps in services for LGBTTQ families and individuals.[1]

The Conceptual Framework

The conceptual framework is an important aspect of the research question and tells the reader what is meant by the concepts that are part of it. Grinnell, Williams and Unrau (2009) define concepts as ideas that need clarification, and in any research question, there are a number of key concepts that need a detailed explanation. Some are relatively straightforward, while others are much more complex. For instance, if we wanted to do a profile of a given community, we may be interested in identifying basic demographic data, such as average years of education and income levels. In this example, the key concepts are years of education and income, both of which are relatively easy to define. On the other hand, in a study of the relationship between poverty and crime, the three key elements of the conceptual framework are poverty, crime and the relationship between the two. There exist several definitions of poverty and crime; our task, for the purpose of developing the conceptual framework, is to explain which definitions we have chosen and why. Additionally, and possibly the most challenging, is coming up with an explanation of what we mean by "the relationship between poverty and crime." Do we want to show that there is a positive relationship, such that the higher the poverty rate, the higher the crime rate, or do we want to show that poverty causes crime? Regardless of our question, we need to help the reader understand what we mean by the various concepts and what information we hope the study will provide.

Variables

In the case of quantitative studies, the development of the conceptual framework is a bit more involved as we also need to define the variables. A variable is anything that varies, which means that there must be at least two values per variable. For example, the variable "gender" has been traditionally defined as having only two values — male and female. But we now understand that gender is made up of a range of categories, including transgender and transsexual. In fact a new term has been coined, "cisgender," which pushes the concept of gender farther. Cisgender describes someone whose gender identification matches the sex they were born with and conveys a sense of privilege in this position. The values of the variable for gender could be cisgender and transgender; however, this is only useful if the research participants are familiar with the terms.

Since quantitative studies involve the analysis of numerical data, the next step is to decide upon value labels for each variable. Education, for example, could include grade school, high school, college or university. We could have four values: 1 for grade school, 2 for high school, 3 for college and

4 for university. Because the variable income is already in numerical form, we simply state the actual amount.

If our study involves an explanatory design and we are hoping to show that there is a causal relationship between two variables, we would need to identify the independent (causal) variable and the dependent (outcome) variable. In program evaluations studies, the program would be the independent variable and the effect on clients would the dependent variable.

Hypothesis

The final step in the development of the conceptual framework in a quantitative study is the identification of the research hypothesis, which is a statement that is testable. There are generally two types of hypotheses: a directional hypothesis and a non-directional hypothesis. A directional hypothesis predicts the type of relationship between the two variables. In the case of a program evaluation, a directional hypothesis could be that clients who attended program x will score higher on characteristic y than clients who did not attend the program. In the case of a non-directional hypothesis, we believe that variable x will affect clients but are not sure in what direction, that is to say, whether clients will score higher or lower on variable y.

The Theoretical Framework

Another important aspect of the development of the research question is the theoretical framework. Theory guides and informs our research. No research is conducted in a theoretical vacuum. Even if we are not immediately aware of our theoretical framework, we always have some basic orientation that influences how we approach the research. The challenge is to identify what that is. This is why reflexive exercises are so important, as they help to situate ourselves within the research. More and more, researchers self-identify in terms of race, class, gender, sexual orientation, education, physical ableness, etc. because these characteristics all contribute to their basic theoretical orientation. As structural social work researchers, we would add the fact that we adhere to a structural theoretical orientation and anti-oppressive principles. If we were conducting a program evaluation for a women's shelter, we would most likely base our research on a feminist theoretical framework. On the other hand, if we were carrying out an evaluation of a behavioural program in a school setting, we would probably choose social learning theory as our framework. Figure 4-1 illustrates how important utilizing theory is in the process of conducting research.

In the example about evaluating a woman's shelter, a feminist perspective is the theory that influences the research design. The researcher is more likely to choose a qualitative method for data collection and interview women who use the shelter. The researcher will then explore the themes that the women

Figure 4-1 The Process of Community-Based Research

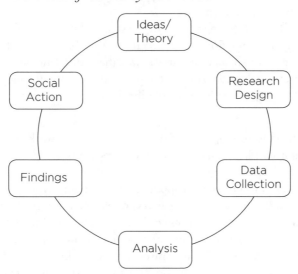

discuss in their interviews. The findings may show that the shelter is seriously underfunded, which has an impact on the safety of the women living there. The research coming from a feminist theoretical perspective would then consider what social action practices could be employed to publicize this serious problem and press for increased funding. The research findings and the subsequent social action will then add to the theory base and influence future research.

Below is an example of the theory that guided the methodological approach used by the group of students mentioned earlier.

> The research approach for this project will be drawing on several theories including anti-oppressive research approach, queer and feminist theory. Anti-oppressive principles suggest that research should be used towards broader social changes, involving the community that is being researched and their potential allies. By interviewing anti-violence service providers on their capacity, knowledge, comfort levels and gaps in providing services to LGBTTQ persons experiencing intimate partner violence, we hope to incite and inspire change in including LGBTTQ persons in anti-violence discourse.
>
> As a group of women conducting research, we are also using a feminist approach in rejecting heteronormative assumptions, concepts and research questions (Kreuger and Neuman 2006). Feminist research calls for "sensitivity to how relations of gender and power permeate all spheres of social life"; thus our research implement takes into account questions of gender, power and

sexuality as it relates to social services (Kreuger and Neuman 2006: 90).

Finally, we are drawing on queer research methodology, which according to Haraway "relies on conversation, connection and an open-ended forum where 'objects' of inquiry become the Subjects of their world and where the agency of the people studied itself transforms the entire project of producing social theory" (cited in Hammers and Brown 2004: 96). Hammers and Brown view such qualitative methods as more appropriate than positivist approaches to research in a queer context.

The Literature Review

As a key part of developing a research question and conceptual and theoretical frameworks, researchers need to consult the existing literature on the topic — i.e., do what is called a "literature review." The literature review is a systematic examination and assessment of the publications available on the topic of interest. Regardless of the nature of the study, it is important to become familiar with the range of research that has already been done. We need to understand what is known about our topic, what gaps exist in our knowledge and how our study will add to the knowledge. If previous research has been done on our question, we may choose to replicate the study or to look at the gaps that still exist and change the question accordingly.

In a university course setting, a research question is often assigned, but if not, the literature is a good source for questions. Most studies conclude with suggestions for further research. Otherwise, issues from practice and involvement with community groups will often be the impetus for general research questions, which can be refined through a literature review (as well as in dialogue with community partners, as we discuss in the next chapter).

Connecting theory to the question may be fairly clear in pure research. In applied research, it may not be so obvious. Practice evaluations require looking at the underlying theory of the practice. For program evaluations, the program may be based on a specific theory. In needs assessments, look at the underlying theories explaining the problem being investigated.

Accessing Information

While many agencies have their own libraries, the best sources of information are most likely the public and university libraries. Library catalogues are computerized, and searches require identification of the author, title or subject, or some combination of these. More and more information is now available on the internet. This is especially true for government documents. Learn how to use the internet efficiently as many hours can be wasted in useless surfing. Marlow (2005: 54–55) offers the following suggestions to help ensure that searches will be productive:

1. State the topic, limit the range, and list all the relevant synonyms and keywords.
2. Use the computer catalogue in your library and identify the keywords to access information.
3. When you access a relevant item, look at its subject headings and use these keywords to access further items.
4. If relevant, locate other materials in government documents.
5. Use keywords to search the online databases available through your library.
6. Use a print index if you have not found enough results in databases.
7. Consult lists of references for further resources.
8. Use gateway sites on the web to track other materials. Verify the source of the web-based information and evaluate it for accuracy, currency and integrity.
9. If the identified material is not available locally or on the web, use interlibrary loans.
10. Ask a reference librarian for other ideas and help, if you need it, for each of these steps.

Writing the Literature Review

The literature review places the current study in its historical and theoretical context. It describes the background to the study and the relationship between the present study and previous studies conducted in the same area. Therefore, cite only research that is specifically pertinent to the current study. Be selective and avoid reviewing or referring to sections of articles or texts that are not related to the study. Discuss and evaluate the selected literature and show the logical continuity between the existing literature and the study. This is discussed in fuller detail in Chapter Twelve, on writing the report.

DISCUSSION QUESTIONS

1. Provide at least four sources of possible research questions
2. Is it possible to conduct structural social work research using a positivist approach? Explain.
3. Explain the difference between exploratory, descriptive and explanatory questions.
4. Why is it important to have a theoretical framework?
5. What should be included in a conceptual framework?
6. Explain the purpose of the literature review.

Note

1. C. Brohman, B. Clancy, J. Dwyer, H. McGechie, A. Vander Kooy, "Intimate Partner Violence Research Proposal," 2010.

5. Research Partners

A crucial aspect of social work research is the identification of research partners. Traditionally, research partners have been referred to as "stakeholders." Some people find this term to be too reflective of corporate/capitalist language. For example, Bonnie Yegidis et al. (2009: 286) define stakeholders as "anyone who has a 'stake' (an investment) in a program and its success." They mention donors, taxpayers, board members, staff members, government regulators and "of course, we cannot forget the clients." Instead, researchers involved in community-based research refer to "community partners" or "community members" (Strand et al. 2003a). Rejecting the term "stakeholders" is one step towards ending the reproduction of dominance. We prefer the term "research partners," which is more reflective of the reciprocal nature of the relationship.

Identifying research partners is particularly important when researchers are exploring sensitive topics (Renzetti and Lee 1993) or when the research potentially has an impact on a population with a history of oppression (Sin 2007). Rather than treating clients as an afterthought, we believe that social work research carried out from a structural perspective should put the interests of the clients first, just as this is our first concern in practice. Furthermore, social work research should be a partnership between researchers and clients. A key principle in AOP is that "participatory approaches between practitioners and clients are necessary" (Baines 2007: 21). Therefore, while it is important to identify all research partners and their respective agendas, we place the clients and their interests ahead of all others.

Another important principle of AOP is that "social work needs to build allies with social causes and movements" (Baines 2007: 21). As we identify all possible research partners, we need to determine potential allies in the structural change process. An example of where the research partners were committed to the change process was a project carried out by two of our master of social work students. The research, which followed a participatory action research (PAR) approach, evaluated a program to help people living with serious mental health problems gain financial autonomy by learning to use banking services. The research partners included, first and foremost, the clients, as well as mental health workers, representatives from a local bank and the researchers, who were all included in a research advisory committee. The committee met weekly and was involved in every aspect of the research. All members of the committee became allies in the change process. They were fully committed to the research and supported the project as well as the participation of those client representatives who were involved in conducting interviews and analyzing the data.

Who Are the Research Partners?

Research partners are the persons affected by an intervention and/or research. They also may include research participants, members of social service organizations, members of the community and members of the university community. Research participants, formerly called subjects, are those persons who provide information through interviews, surveys, observations, focus groups and/or documents. Clients or service users are those persons who receive social service interventions. Community members are persons who belong to the community affected by the intervention and the evaluation. These categories are not mutually exclusive; an individual may be a research participant, service user and community member simultaneously. Service user involvement is actively sought in participatory action research and other forms of community-based research. Their role may be collaborative, where the research is conducted in partnership between the researcher and the service user, and/or consultative, where the consultation is initiated by the service user and there is an equitable distribution of power (Fox, Martin and Green 2007).

Research partners associated with the social service organization may include the board of directors, administrators, social workers and other staff, and clients and consumers of the services, as well as the community. Boards of directors are persons elected by constituency groups or appointed to oversee the administration of the organization. Board members often include users of the services provided by the organization. For example, an evaluation of a seniors drop-in program at a community health and resource centre could involve working with the centre's board of directors. In such a project, the same elder could be a community member, service user and a member of the board.

Funders are those individuals who represent the source of financing and, thus, have input into the parameters of the research. They could have an impact on needs assessments or other types of applied research by directing the researchers to look at one group of potential service users over another. For example, an organization wanting to find out the needs of a new immigrant group, so they can adjust their services to be more welcoming, may have to choose one of a number of groups to survey. Funders may influence this decision directly or indirectly if they can only provide funding for particular services or a particular group. Public, provincial or municipal funding bodies will have their own political agenda, and private funding bodies also have "political" agendas and interests in the organizations they fund. Funding can also come from private-public partnerships. Most hospitals have private foundations that contribute to their funding.

Agency administrators, for example, the executive director, are those persons hired by the board to oversee to the day-to-day administration of the organization. Social workers are responsible for implementing the interventions, and they are often helped by other frontline staff, their supervisors and, at times, the agency research coordinator.

In community-university research partnerships, there are also research partners associated with the university. These include students, social work research course instructors, the research ethics board and the school of social work. Student researchers collaborate in the design and implementation of the collection and analysis of information of a research project. Students generally work in collaboration with agency representatives. In the case of the course we teach, small groups of students select to work together on a specific project. Of course we, as course instructors who supervise the students conducting the research projects, are also research partners. We have concerns about the quality of student learning and maintaining the reputation of the school as a research institution. The university REB (which we

Figure 5-1 Relationship between University and Community Research Partners

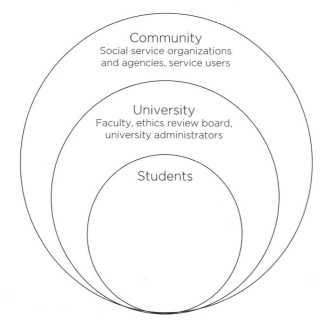

Figure 5-2 An Example of the Relationship between Community Research Partners

discussed in Chapter Three) is one research partner whose concern is with protecting the rights of research participants. Figure 5.1 shows the relationships between the community, the university and students and emphasizes the fact that students are also members of the community with whom they are in partnership.

It can be helpful to create a diagram of the relationships between research partners to help get a clearer idea of the inter-relationships involved. Social workers often use a tool called a genogram, which maps family structures, to help practioners understand family dynamics (McGoldrick, Gerson and Shellenberger 1999). The example in Figure 5.2 shows the relationship between the partners involved in a research project exploring what community houses can do to better serve community members. Some of the questions they attempted to answer were: what was working well for tenant associations in this neighbourhood? What kind of additional supports do tenant associations need? What role can community houses play in better supporting tenant associations? The research team created this picture to better understand the relationships between the research partners.

Research Partners and Their Agendas

One important step in preparing for community-based research is to determine the relevant research partners, what particular issues are of importance to them and how much power they have in the decision-making process. Not all of the possible research partners listed above will have an apparent role in every research or evaluation project. Some partners may have an indirect (less obvious) influence, but they may still have a major impact on the research.

Conflict among research partners, while uncommon, can come at a cost to the research project. Conflicts vary from disagreements over logistical aspects of the research to disparity in fundamental values and principles. Conflicts may arise because one research partner exercises power in a manner that negatively affects the research process. It is important to think through the roles and agendas of the research partners ahead of time in an effort to diffuse some of the potential sources of conflict. A list of social work skills that are helpful to employ in case of conflict is included later in this chapter. The following are comments from a student's reflexive journal:

> I had to do some serious soul searching to see how I felt about conducting social work research within the context of the medical model (of which I have always been critical). Several additional challenges came about in relation to the research environment, including costs (of materials, parking), scheduling conflicts (for meetings, deadlines, etc.), communication and departmental conflicts. An example of this was when the process of our project was challenged by a staff member feeling threatened by what they perceived to be an evaluation of their programming. While these issues remain sensitive, I believe our group alleviated this tension by (a) clarifying our neutrality as researchers, and (b) agreeing to delay our abstract submission to the conference, so that the results could first be reviewed by hospital administration. Personally, I see this selectivity of dissemination as highly political and oppressive, and this decision very much conflicted with my notions of academic integrity.[1]

Organizational research partners can have various possible agendas. Administrators may be concerned that research returning negative results might jeopardize their funding. In one of our earlier studies, the administrators did not want their employees' union to receive the results for fear of them being used in upcoming negotiations. In a more recent study, an organization's executive director wanted to be the only one to see the results of the study. The organization had unsuccessfully gone through accreditation, and the director was concerned about staff morale and thus wanted to control the flow of information. Another community organization director told students that she "only wanted to see positive quotes." It is important to understand the stress that community organizations experience in the current economic climate of funding cutbacks, but it is also important to incorporate ethical research methods into the study design.

While a university is not directly involved with students' research projects, their indirect interest in the work should not be overlooked. Our university has supported our approach to teaching research, but each time a group of students goes into the community, the university's reputation is "on the line." At worst, if the research goes awry and clients or community groups are adversely affected, there is always the potential for a lawsuit. Several years ago, we had received a small research grant to study child poverty in a small Ontario city. We started by creating a research network made up of four equal partner organizations: the Social Planning Council, the Regional Health Unit, the city and the university. Each partner organization was to send one representative to make up the research team, with us representing the university. The team agreed to base the study on the latest census data and to develop recommendations on how child poverty levels could be improved as well as how to support low-income families. After several months of work, the team was ready to release its report. We printed a hundred copies of the report with the logos of the four partner organizations printed on the front cover. We scheduled a press conference, and each partner organization received an advance copy of the report a week before the conference. A day before the press conference, we received a call from the director of the city's Health and Welfare Department insisting that we could not release the report with the city's logo on the cover because the city council had not approved the recommendations. We argued in vain that the plan all along was to include recommendations and that the representative of the city had helped to develop them, but the director would not budge. We were forced to remove all the covers and have new ones printed. The representative from the city on our team was ordered to stop attending and a new representative was appointed. The incident reminded me once again that research is not apolitical.

We should also point out that not all social workers are supportive of research. A worker whose program is being evaluated may question the necessity for the evaluation. They may interpret any evaluation as being a critique of their performance and try to find ways to limit the scope of the study. Researchers need to be sensitive to these concerns when communicating the aims of the project with agency staff.

During the first meeting, the role of the social work researcher is to make all research agendas explicit and to negotiate a plan of action with partners around how the research will proceed. Most research partners will have their own perspectives on the project and will have a strong input on agenda setting. Service users may feel that they have the least power and research expertise of any member of the team. They may need to be supported. One way to do this is to emphasize the value of their lived experience and the contribution this will make to the research process. Part of the student agenda is ensuring the project can be completed successfully within the academic year and that it provides a useful service to clients.

Students conducting community-based research are inclined to focus on achieving high grades, want to publish research results to further their careers, are concerned about their reputation in the community and often hope to be employed by the community agency with which they are collaborating. This combination can result in students perceiving themselves as lacking power in negotiations with the community agency. Seifer (2006) discusses the need to balance power among partners and build community and campus capacity to engage each other as equals. One example of an imbalance of power was a project where students were asked to survey employees in a large city organization after there had been a labour dispute that resulted in a strike. The management did not want the survey results to be distributed to the union. They wanted to decide on a strategy to address the concerns that employees raised without input from the union. The students did not feel comfortable with this as they had promised their research participants that they would be able to see the results. The students also knew that for the employees to have any power to make the changes they had suggested in the survey that the labour union had to be appraised of the results. They took a great risk and leaked the survey results to the union.

Community organizations often see the university as controlling the research process. Historically, university faculty would design, fund and execute their research agendas with little input from the community. The results would be analyzed and often not reported to the community at all, or if a report was given to community members or research participants, it was not written in language that was easily accessible. This is one of the reasons why First Nations people adopted the OCAP principles, which we discuss further in Chapter Seven.

Table 5.1 can help any of the research partners evaluate what might be different agendas among the partners and how much power/control they exert in the research process. Understanding these dynamics can help facilitate any difficulties that can come up between research partners.

Negotiating with research partners requires a great deal of sensitivity and tact. Some of the skills taught in social work practice courses in terms of active listening, showing empathy and sessional contracting (Shulman 1999) are useful in these negotiations. Lavoie, MacDonald and Whitmore (2010: 304) identify the following skills as essential to building relationships that are healthy and share power:

> *Active listening*: By taking the time to "tune in" to peoples' daily struggles (Shulman 2006), the researcher can learn about the role of the family, culture, history and politics in individuals' lives (Lundy 2004). This helps researchers identify the potential barriers to participation as well as those features of daily life that

Table 5-1 Research Partner Power Dynamics – Ottawa Example

Research Partners	Power/Control	Agenda
Client or consumer groups (current and future)	N/A	N/A
Participants	Possibly discredit research and influence recommendations.	Safeguarding their programming, organizational and personal reputation. To increase programming in order to meet client's needs.
Advisory group (made up of clients and organizational representatives)	They could discredit our work within the Muslim community.	Safeguarding community and community needs.
Organizational administrators	By commissioning the research we are accountable to working within the organization's framework.	Be able to seek funding for additional programming and to create community partnerships. Also to increase organizational reputation within marginalized communities.
Organizational staff	N/A	N/A
Research team	Responsible for design to dissemination of research. Able to manipulate data and participants' responses to fit our themes.	To receive a high grade within the course. The researchers also want to build credibility, reputation and networking within the broader Ottawa community.
Course instructors	Responsible for grading the research project. Affects grades and marks of the researchers. The instructor also provides supervision and guidelines as per university standards.	To maintain and increase reputation of the master of social work program within the Ottawa community. To provide students with the experience of linking theory to practice within the research field.
The university (ethics board)	The research ethics board has the most power in this research because we need their approval to proceed with any projects.	To protect the health and wellbeing of participants and students.
Funding body (if any)	N/A	N/A
The general community (Ottawa Muslim community)	The community is able to discredit research results.	To ensure that the research results accurately reflect the needs and wants of the community.

Source: Adapted from McNulty et al. 2009.

constrain and empower research partnerships.

Relationship-building: Relationships based on respect, clear boundaries and power-sharing are necessary in order for people to work together in an egalitarian way and to sustain the research process (Redmond 2005). Communication skills, including clarifying, summarizing, questioning and empathy, help to make this possible (Carniol 2003).

Facilitation: Like social work, the research moves forward by facilitating a process of decision-making, group sharing, learning and collective action (Finn 2004). The goal of facilitation is a space for self-expression and dialogue that considers power differentials in the group and ensures that all voices are heard (Mullaly 2002).

Critical reflection: Critical reflection is necessary to understand how judgements and preconceptions reproduce relations of power (Chiu 2006). This includes an awareness of our own positioning along the lines of ability, sexual orientation, gender, class, race and other social divisions in order to understand and confront the power relations intrinsic to practice (Fook 2002a).

Advocacy: Ideally, the researcher accompanies participants, who advocate for themselves. If participants are unable to represent themselves, however, a participatory researcher may act as advocate on behalf of community members with service delivery organizations and policy-makers for access to better services, for example (Ristock and Pennell 1996).

Being an ally: The researcher serves as an ally to oppressed groups by taking a stand against injustice (Dullea 2006). As in social Work practice (Bishop 1994), this includes putting personal power at the disposal of the group, engaging in social action in support of research participants and building solidarity amongst groups that share social justice concerns.

In our research course, we found that instructors need to be part of initial negotiations. Recognizing that students have little or no power when it comes to determining the scope of the research, our role as instructors during these negotiations is to keep the expectations realistic and approve only those projects that are manageable within the limits of the course and the academic year.

The following helpful tips come from the work of Carl Brun (2005). First, just as social workers negotiate the scope of the intervention with their clients, social work researchers should do the same with research partners. Describe in detail all the tasks to be carried out and by whom. Examples include the methods to be used in contacting participants, data collection and analysis, the expected uses of the results, the distribution of the final report, who owns the data once the project is completed and authorship of paper presentations and journal articles. If there are costs involved, discuss fees and other potential miscellaneous costs. All of the decisions resulting from these negotiations should be put in the form of a contract to be signed by both parties.

Second, the research partners and the researchers should discuss any potential conflicts of interest. Social work researchers who come from a structural perspective will need to be up front about their orientation and their research values. If the organization cannot support a structural orientation, it may be better not to proceed with the research. When working with community groups, personal conflicts within the group might have an impact on the ease of conducting research. Also, if the organization requesting the research states that continued funding or the accreditation of their organization depends upon a positive research outcome, the researchers need to state explicitly that they cannot guarantee this. A potential conflict-of-interest situation occurs when the social work researchers are also employees, field placement students or volunteers at the organization being evaluated.

Third, keep in close communication with direct research partners. Invariably, the original design will need to be changed once the research project is under way. Timelines may need to be altered, access to participants may not work out as planned, and there may be turnover of staff or researchers. Alterations to the original contract should be negotiated as the need arises. To facilitate this process, researchers should keep a detailed journal of the research activities.

Finally, researchers need to ensure that results are reported accurately. While the researchers and their partners have an interest in uncovering findings that will support positive social change, the team must accept that this may not be the case. There may be events over the course of the research that will limit how much can be disclosed with respect to interpretations of the results. For instance, there may have been a poor participant response rate or problems with the administration of the research. These limitations need to be discussed with research partners and included in the final report.

When working in small groups with other research participants to design and implement a research project it is helpful to keep the following in mind:

1. *Communication*:
    a. Decide at the very beginning how often and in what manner you will communicate with each other.
    b. It is sometimes helpful to designate one person to directly communi-

cate with the research group members or research partners rather than each group member sending many emails.

c. Check out your assumptions about the other people in your research group and their motivations. If you have service users as members of your research group, do not make assumptions about their level of expertise in conducting research.

d. Don't let things fester; bring up issues as they come up.

e. Setting up a joint email account for the research group is sometimes helpful.

f. Make sure one person proofreads any written material for consistency in writing and grammar if many group members have contributed to it.

2. *Distribution of Tasks*:

a. Some research groups like to ensure that each member experiences all aspects of the research process while other groups prefer to divide tasks according to the different skill sets of each member. Either way is perfectly acceptable. You should decide this at the beginning of your interactions.

3. *Roles*:

Each person in a group feels most comfortable assuming a particular role. A group with too many leaders or too many followers will have a hard time functioning. It can be helpful to talk about distribution of the roles. Many groups rotate the leadership or note-taking role, etc. so that everyone can take a turn at the different roles.

The Research Partners' Plan

Before the actual research begins, the social work researchers should create a research partners' plan. Carl Brun (2005: 43–44) states that the plan should identify the major groups of research partners and what is expected from each. The first such group is made up of those people requesting the research. Is it the client or community group, the organization that is providing the programs or the funders who are interested in the research question?

The second major group of research partners is the research advisory committee. This committee oversees the planning and implementation of the research. While not every research project will involve an advisory committee, projects that follow a structural approach, whereby clients have maximum input, must include such a committee. The committee should be made up of clients or community representatives, representatives from the organization and possibly representatives from the board of directors and funders.

The following is a student group description of their advisory committee for a research project with the Muslim community:

To ensure that we are truly engaging in anti-oppressive social work research, our intention is to implement the following three practices into our research process:

(1) use a faith based advisory committee whose main goal will be to help ensure that our interview questions and research study methodologies are culturally appropriate;

(2) engage, as researchers, in what Potts and Brown (2005) call political listening (i.e., which involves "being open and perceptive, interpreting and judging" during both the data collection and analysis phases of research (Potts and Brown 2005: 272);

(3) involve the participants in the review of the proposed recommendations of the research project so as to ensure that what has been proposed as recommendations/next steps reflect the values of the participants The research team is awaiting ethics approval before setting up this committee; however we are looking at recruiting representatives from the following community organizations known to provide services to the Muslim community.[2]

The third major group is the researcher or research team. This is the group that will carry out the actual research. In the above example, it includes the student research team and the instructor supervising the students. In the case of PAR, the research team may include clients or community members.

The Research Question

Research partners directly influence all phases of the research, even the initial phase of the process — choosing the research question. In our research course, usually the organizational partners submit a "request for research" with one or more research questions already listed. Unfortunately, it is rare that their clients initiate this process, and, in most cases, clients are not consulted on the nature of the research or the choice of questions.

The types of questions that organizations typically propose are, for example: What is the effectiveness of program x? or What are the needs of client group y? or Is client group z satisfied with programs a, b or c? Referring to the information in Table 5-1, the research team should try to identify who controls the research and the agenda behind the research question.

At times, organizations are upfront with the team about their motivation. For instance, a few organizations have admitted to us that their programs are up for re-accreditation and they need research to support their application. At other times, organizational research partners may not be quite so open. Directors concerned about shrinking budgets may be looking for justification to discontinue a program and hope to use research to show that it is not cost-effective.

If a client group initiates the research process but is unclear about an appropriate research question, the research team might suggest organizing a focus group. These groups are generally made up of six to ten "typical" clients of the organization. The group, with the help of a research team member acting as a facilitator, can engage in a "brainstorming" session, with the goal of developing a research question that clients agree will meet their needs. Clients who also sit on the board of the organizations may be able to suggest areas of research arising from their board responsibilities.

The way the research question is framed is very important. Below are two examples of different ways to view a research question and how that influences the methodology:

1. *Agency Administration*: Are we in the Community Integration Program achieving our community-based organization objectives, are we meeting funder objectives, as well as fulfilling the expectations of our strategic plan?
2. *Agency Social Worker*: Is our organization achieving its goal of being a community-based organization and meeting the expectations of the people we serve and the community organizations that we network and partner with?

If the first research question is selected, the research might include documenting the amount of time that social workers spend in various activities, surveying funders and creating a logic model (discussed in a later chapter) to evaluate if the goals of the strategic plan are being met. If the latter question is asked, the research might survey clients and community partners to assess their views on how well the organization is meeting their expectations.

The Initial Meeting

The initial meeting between the organization and the research team should be used as an opportunity to bring agendas out in the open. As stated earlier, members of the research team may need to use a great deal of tact to help organizational research partners open up about their motivation for requesting the research. Any concerns the organization may have (about possible outcomes of the research, who owns the data, the dissemination of results, etc.) should be discussed during this initial meeting.

The role of clients should be discussed at the initial meeting. Even if the organization had not initially planned to involve clients, the research team should encourage this. For instance, they could propose an advisory committee, whose role would be to oversee the research process, made up of client and organizational representatives. The research team members should discuss the advantages and disadvantages of involving clients in all phases of the research. The advantages are, of course, that this will give clients maximum control of the research. The main disadvantages, discussed in the previous chapter, are issues of anonymity and confidentiality.

Choosing a Methodology

An important decision point in the research process is the choice of methods. Since, in our experience, most requests for research come from social work organizations rather than client groups, it is generally the organizational research partners who direct and approve the methodology. This includes the selection of participants, the forms of data collection and the method of analysis.

Here again, social work researchers should make organizational research partners aware of the advantages of involving clients in the choice of methods. For instance, clients can be helpful in the selection of participants. They may be willing to informally spread the word about the research and the potential benefits to clients. They could also be helpful in choosing instruments for data collection. They may point out flaws with an instrument that are not immediately obvious to the researchers or organizational representatives, for instance that the language used is too scholarly or involves too much social work jargon. There are many questions that new immigrants would not address in a focus group format. These participants will be hesitant to answer personal questions that expose areas of problems in their families in front of other members of their community. We have been advised to use individual interviews to get answers to these kinds of questions. Pre-testing the instrument on a small sample of clients could also be invaluable in terms of ensuring, for example, the questions on the interview guide are clear and relevant to clients. If clients are involved in the data analysis, they may have insights that are unavailable to researchers who are viewing the data from outside the community.

The Research Report

The research report should be written with the audience in mind. If the report is being disseminated to an audience of administrative research partners, the language used in the report can be quite technical. On the other hand, if the report is intended for client research partners, it should be written in more accessible language. A good way to ensure the report is useful to client research partners is to share a draft report with a client advisory group and obtain feedback. Incorporating suggested revisions of the client advisory group will ensure the final report is as useful as possible. Writing the research report is discussed further in Chapter Twelve.

Community-Based Research

There is a growing body of literature around the challenges inherent in universities and communities engaging in community-based research (CBR). CBR seeks to democratize knowledge by validating multiple sources of information and promoting multiple methods of discovery and dissemination, with the goal of social action (Strand et al. 2003b). Some of the challenges of conduction CBR include insufficient funding (Seifer and Calleson 2004; Savan 2004), systemic barriers in the academy (Ahmed, Maurana and Newton 2004), university time lines (Hyde and Meyer 2004), monitoring whether the research is truly community initiated and driven (Flicker, Savan, McGrath, Kolenda and Mildenberger 2007; Minkler 2004, 2005), negotiating memoranda of understanding ([MOUs] a written agreement between the research partners) and research protocols (Minkler 2004; Moretti, Leadbeater and Marshall 2006), managing the ethics review process (Boser 2006) and negotiating ownership and dissemination of the research results (Seifer and Calleson 2004). Conceptualizing university–community research projects as community-based research brings us a slightly different set of assumptions and makes the actual process more transparent.

Engaged scholarship is defined by Timothy Stanton (2008) as research that partners university scholarly resources with those in the public and private sectors to enrich knowledge, address and help solve critical social issues and contribute to social justice. For high-quality engaged scholarship, engagement must take place in the development of the purpose, throughout the research process and in the compilation of the research product. In relation to purpose, Stanton (2008) evaluates quality in terms of whether the purpose of the research is to benefit the community, directly or indirectly, and whether the findings are intended to "work in particular contexts with particular people to achieve a particular purpose" (24). He proposes engaging in a level of collaboration that is sufficient or appropriate at each stage of the research process. In terms of product, Stanton (2008) envisions a range of products, where the results lead to concrete action, changed practice, changed policies and various communication vehicles, including academic, popular and community specific publications.

Cheryl Hyde and Megan Meyer (2004) conceptualize a continuum from participatory action to conventional research, with most CBR projects situated somewhere along the continuum. They claim that a variety of factors affect the participatory nature of a project, including the nature of the problem to be explored, the skill and training of the researcher, the environmental context and the desires of the community. Stoecker (2003) notes that the "community could be social service agencies rather than grass root residents, and collaboration could simply mean obtaining approval for a researcher-defined project" (36).

McDonald (2007) conceptualizes a slightly different continuum. She uses the term community-engaged to portray a spectrum of approaches that involve the community in the research process. Her continuum includes research that incorporates only a few elements of community-engagement, for example, having external, often university based, researchers control the research with the community in a more consultative role at one end. At the other end is research in which community members and outside or external researchers are equal partners throughout the process. The extent of the collaboration differs from project to project. The students in our course have undertaken research projects situated at different points along this continuum.

Universities have incorporated community-based research as a means to engage the community and educate students, though the literature shows different benefits depending on how it is used. Community-based research has been incorporated into research courses (Anderson 2002; Hyde and Meyer 2004; Stuart and Whitmore 2006; Peters and Gray 2007); other course work (e.g., environmental studies and political science courses at Carleton University use a form of CBR as service learning) (Bzruzy and Segal 1996; Bird, Ambiee and Kuzin 2007; Andrée 2008); non-course connected student research assistantships with community agencies (Savan 2004); and collaborations through a university-based community partnership centre (Rogge and Rocha 2004). When CBR is incorporated into a research course, one of the major benefits is giving students a hands-on research experience (Chapdelaine and Chapman 1999; Hyde and Meyer 2004). A number of studies have shown positive outcomes for students from these initiatives, including creating a greater appreciation for research (Strand 2000; Eyler et al. 2001; Hayes 2006).

Some scholars argue that the more collaborative the research process is between university and community partners the more effective it can be, both as scholarship and as service to society (Arches 2007; Stanton 2008). Flicker (2008) found that there were benefits in engaging in community-based participatory research (CBR) in terms of the quality of the research and sense of accomplishment of the research partners (including community members). However, the costs of engaging in CBPR included extra time to complete projects, extra burden on overloaded research partners and confusion around decision-making.

Karen Schwartz (2010) conducted a study of some of the projects undertaken by students in our course. Several themes emerged from the community organizations about the benefits and drawbacks of these partnerships. The benefits included the concrete ways that the organizations made use of the research reports they received and the exchange of knowledge, skill and technology. The drawbacks included difficulties in communication that led to issues of power and control between the partners, students and instructors. The community contact people were generally content with the quality of the relationship with the university and students. They appreciated the instructor attending the first meeting. Respondents stated that "it was helpful to clarify the nuances of each [partner's] perspective"; that the meeting "laid the groundwork for the project" and "got [us] talking about concrete things that the students wanted to research and to set limits on the students (not enough time to interview a hundred people)."

The community contact people also generally felt that the research produced was useful to the organization. All of the participating organizations made use of some or all of the information in the final report from the students, thus achieving Stanton's (2008) standard of quality engaged research. Several stated that they would integrate the information into funding applications. Others responded that they planned to use the findings to create new programs or in staff and volunteer training. Some organizations incorporated the data into conference presentations, and one organization planned to use the data to refine its program. One research project was featured on a local radio show. The students were interviewed and publicized the work of the organization, the results of their research and the needs of black youth in the public school system. Two years later, a new program that had been established as a result of this research was publicized on the same radio program. Examples of some of the responses about the use of the findings are as follows:

> We will be using the findings in our application for funding from the ministry."

> We will take the results to the volunteers to discuss what can be done to address the challenges raised.

> The literature review was helpful because we received up to date information on why we are doing what we are doing.

The organization contact people were asked for suggestions for improving the collaboration and the research process. Some of the research participants felt that there were communication difficulties. These suggestions depended on where the project fell on the continuum of participatory and conventional research. A couple of respondents said: "We would have wanted more check-ins with the students" and suggested including a more detailed schedule of meetings with students in the initial contract. Other comments related to a desire for greater input: "We would have liked more input in the development of the final report; We would have liked more discussion on the interpretation of the data." This comment is particularly noteworthy as it differs from previous studies in which community organizations did not want such input because they felt it would bias the analysis (Hyde and Meyer 2004). This highlights tensions in community-engaged research not previously discussed in the literature. Community partners may start at one point on Hyde and Meyer's (2004) continuum of engagement and may move to wanting to be more or less involved as the research proceeds. Some partners became increasingly concerned about the unfavourable results from the program evaluation and how funders might view these. In addition, the critical analysis that is emphasized in academia can be threatening for some community partners.

The following is a comment from the general feedback section:

> Students from the MSW program have been involved in this program from its inception in 2006. They have assisted in its design, in the creation of the wellness manual, in the running of the sessions, and in its evaluation. A research group completed a more formal program evaluation of the wellness sessions. Without the participation of the School of Social Work, I think we never would have come this far in the program development for this award winning project. (Schwartz 2010: 7)

Figure 5-3 lists the benefits that students, the community and the instructors felt they gained by participation in CBR.

One of our community partners identified the following benefits of engaging in CBR:
1. being able to evaluate their practice as social workers;
2. getting students' and professors' input into how they could evaluate their practice
3. the morale boost from students' enthusiasm;
4. having students move the research forward when they did not have time;
5. the collection of data
6. having fun;
7. building research knowledge and expertise;
8. supporting/coaching others to enable them to feel more confident in their research skills.

The challenges included the following:
1. taking on too many projects at one time;
2. taking on projects that involve a great deal of data collection;
3. research course constraints;
4. social workers' time constraints;

Figure 5.3 Benefits of Community-Based Research

Student	Instructor	Community Partner
• Develop research skills • If not doing a thesis, have something in CV related to engaging in research • Develop relationship with agency • Employment with agency • Improve employment opportunities in general • Conference presentations • Media exposure	• Publications and conference presentations • Contribution to community agencies • Teaching students how to do research in the real world	• Funding proposals to maintain or improve funding • Documentation for funders of meeting program objectives • Change programs based on information from program evaluation • Volunteer training • Improved relationship with broader community • Media exposure

Source: Schwartz 2010: 10.

5. working with two ethics boards (the hospital's and the university's);
6. the level of rigour/quality; and
7. collaboration dynamics (Nelson, Schwartz and van de Sande 2009).

Another community partner had the following similar ideas about the benefits:

1. increases the profile of social workers as researchers;
2. provides useful information to practitioners;
3. strengthens partnerships between academics and practitioners for the benefit of service users
4. the fewer resources required by from the community agency by research students as opposed to clinical (placement) students; and
5. provides an opportunity to evaluate social work practice in a mental health setting as well as to answer broader questions.

The following challenges were also identified:

1. thinking of a project that students would be interested in and could be completed within the timeframe and other constraints of the course
2. their limited time to supervise research students;
3. their unfamiliarity with the culture of research;
4. working with two ethics boards; and
5. challenging collaboration dynamics (Schwartz, O'Brien and van de Sande 2009).

In this chapter, we discuss the importance of identifying the research partners and their respective agendas. We also consider the benefits of involving clients and suggest ways to include them. We examine the phases of the research process and how research partners might attempt to influence the process during each phase. It is our hope that this chapter helps prepare researchers for the benefits of working collaboratively with community partners as well as the social and political dynamics that could adversely affect research quality.

DISCUSSION QUESTIONS

1. What do you think should be the role of an advisory committee in a research project?
2. Who might be involved in an advisory committee?
3. How much input should they have in creating the research instrument?
4. If members of the advisory committee are also participants in the research, do you foresee difficulties in them being involved in data collection or other phases of the research? Why or why not?
5. How would you handle a situation in which research partners are trying to influence the research in what you deem to be an inappropriate way?

Notes

1. Charles Forlotte, Reflexive Journal, November 2007.
2. J. McNulty, K. Bongard, L. Middleton, G. Arkorful and L. Perron, "Beyond the Absence of Disease: Identifying Barriers, Gaps and Needs in Sexual and Reproductive Health Services Offered to Muslim Youth in the Ottawa Area," unpublished paper, 2009.

6. Participatory Action Research

The research method that best encapsulates the structural approach to research is participatory action research (PAR). While there are a number of variations of participatory research, PAR emphasizes the importance of social justice and empowering people (Marlow 2005; Payne 2005; Rubin and Babbie 2008; Dudley 2010). James Dudley (2010) states that PAR allows the researcher to collaborate with the people affected by the problem on the articulation of the research question and design. He also believes that PAR assists the researchers and participants in determining if the study will bring about social change. He suggests that PAR should involve the participants, who, after a certain amount of training, act as "lay researchers," collaborating on an equal footing with professional researchers, clients and community leaders.

To elaborate, PAR is a participatory process that requires the equal and collaborative involvement of clients in the identification of their concerns and in the search for solutions and actions to address their identified needs and improve their social conditions. The belief is that social research should be more than simply "finding out"; research should also involve an action component that seeks to assist in social justice change. A PAR approach encourages the participation of citizens who are service users and thus have a

Figure 6-1 Participatory Action Research

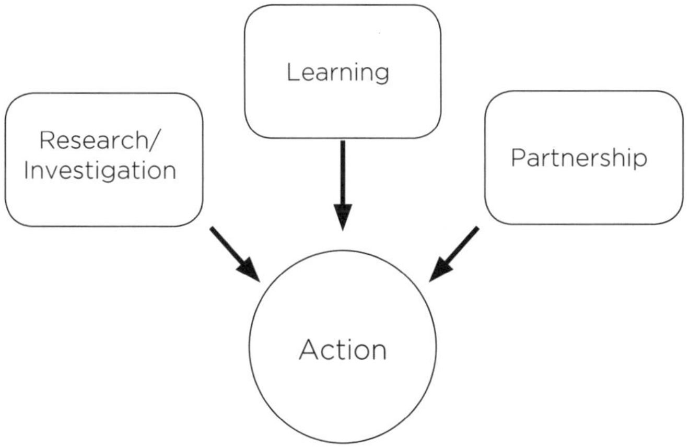

vested interest in the outcomes of the research. PAR promotes independence and can be an essential component to identifying the needs of vulnerable populations (Balcazar, Garcia-Iriarte and Suarez-Balcazar 2009). Figure 6-1 illustrates the importance of the action component of PAR.

The History of Action Research

The term "action research" was first introduced during the early part of the twentieth century by Kurt Lewin. Known as the father of group dynamics, Lewin believed in the active participation of people (Shulman 1999). His work on group dynamics led him to propose a combination of research and action as way to encourage citizen participation in problem solving (Toseland and Rivas 1998).

Citizen participation is not new to social work. The community development literature is full of examples of people identifying their own needs and developing strategies for meeting those needs. Jack Rothman (1979), in his classic work on community organization, identified three models: locality development, social planning and social action. Both locality development and social action involve extensive citizen participation. Rothman defines locality development as a model that "presupposes that community change may be pursued optimally through broad participation of a wide spectrum of people at the local community level in goal determination and action" (26). Rothman adds that the locality development approach was used over a century ago by the settlement houses in Britain and the United States. The social action model, developed primarily by Saul Alinsky, stresses the importance of collective action and the need to organize oppressed people into a political force. In speaking about community organization, Alinsky (1969: 78) stated: "It should always be remembered that a real organization of the people, one in which they completely believe and which they feel is definitely their own, must be rooted in the experiences of the people themselves."

The roots of PAR can be traced back to the work of Paolo Freire (2005) on the importance of critical consciousness. Known for his work on the liberation of oppressed people in Brazil, Freire was the first to make the link between education and political transformation. Freire's definition of education was broader than the traditional sense. In his introduction to Freire's book, *The Politics of Education*, Henry Giroux provides the following explanation:

> For Freire, education includes and moves beyond the notion of schooling. Schools represent only one important site where education takes place, where men and women both produce and are the product of specific social and pedagogical relations. Education represents in Freire's view both a struggle for meaning and a struggle over power relations. (Freire 1985: xii)

In his book *Pedagogy of the Oppressed*, first published in 1970, Freire presents the concept of "praxis," which involves an ongoing cyclical process of planning, action and reflection. PAR involves the use of praxis as a way of developing knowledge and the critical consciousness of community members (Prilleltensky 2001). Freire also warned about the dangers of traditional research:

> The real danger of the investigation is not that the supposed objects of the investigation, discovering themselves to be co-investigators, might "adulterate" the analytical results. On the contrary, the danger lies in the risk of shifting the focus from meaningful themes to the people themselves, thereby treating the people as objects of the investigation. (2005: 107)

Freire explains that traditional research only serves to reinforce the reciprocal and complementary relationship between oppressor and oppressed. Freire sees research not as a neutral act but as an act of solidarity (Hall 2005: 4). Marlyn Bennett (2004), who provides a thorough literature review of PAR, states that although Freire did not actually develop PAR as a specific research method, he would be a strong supporter.

The actual term, participatory action research, originated in the 1970s with Colombian sociologist Orlando Fals-Borda (Fals-Borda and Rahman 1991). In 1977, Fals-Borda helped organize the first conference on PAR, in Cartagena, Colombia. Building on the work of Freire, Fals-Borda and his colleagues chose to use their research skill as an alternative to traditional research and to strengthen political and democratic movements (Hall 2005: 9).

Budd Hall (2005), who was an active participant at the Cartagena conference, describes how he became involved in developing an international network of researchers using PAR. He states that PAR was not readily accepted by certain political regimes and that Maria Christinal Salazar, a Columbian scholar and the wife of Fals-Borda, was detained by police because she was perceived as being too closely connected with groups seeking political change in their country. Hall also writes about the resistance to PAR by his academic colleagues because of the perceived lack of scientific rigour. Nevertheless, by the 1990s, in spite of much resistance, PAR had taken a firm hold in international development (Hall 2005).

In his paper published in the journal *Convergence*, Hall provides the following definitional statement, which was the result of discussions held during the first meeting of the international network at Aurora, Ontario, in 1977. It should be noted that Hall (2005: 12) uses the terms "participatory research" (PR) and "participatory action research" (PAR) interchangeably.

1. PR involves a whole range of powerless groups of people – exploited, the poor, the oppressed, and the marginal.
2. It involves the full and active participation of the community in the entire research process.
3. The subject of the research originates in the community itself and the problem is defined, analyzed and solved by the community.
4. The ultimate goal is the radical transformation of the social reality and the improvement of the lives of the people themselves. The beneficiaries of the research are the members of the community.
5. The process of participatory research can create greater awareness in the people of their own resources and mobilize them for self-reliant development.
6. It is a more scientific method of research in that the participation of the community in the research process facilitates a more accurate and authentic analysis of social reality.
7. The researcher is a committed participant and learner in the process of research, i.e., a militant rather than a detained observer (Hall 2005).

PAR Compared with Traditional Research

Clearly, PAR is quite different from traditional research methods. Baum, MacDougall and Smith (2006: 854) describe three primary differences:

1. Unlike traditional research, PAR involves a cyclical reflective process leading to action. Participants collect and analyze data and determine what action should be taken as a result of the research. This action is then researched using the same reflective process.
2. In traditional research, the researched are the objects of investigation with all decisions made by the researchers. PAR involves power sharing between researchers and the researched. The lines between the two are deliberately blurred until the researched become the researchers. All decisions concerning the research question, the data collection, the analysis, and how the results should be used are taken jointly by the researchers and the researched.
3. Traditional researchers make use of an empiricist approach that separates the data and information from its context, whereas PAR researchers believe that you cannot make sense of the data without considering the context. For instance, feminist empiricists such as Helen Longino (1990) state that scientific evidence should only be conceived in the context of investigating some hypothesis. She believes that scientific knowledge must be viewed within its political, social and cultural context and that scientific knowledge is social knowledge and can be achieved only by individuals working in a community context.

Table 6-1 Researcher as Facilitator

The Researcher	The Facilitator of Research
The inquiry is the researcher's inquiry.	The inquiry is more or less the participants' inquiry.
The research partners are the researcher's subjects, or the recipients of the researcher's final report.	The research partners are participants and co-researchers with the facilitator.
The researcher usually conducts an on-off, time limited inquiry, implementing a research plan established and agreed at the outset.	The facilitator assists an iterative, emergent inquiry that might be more or less continuous and responsive. Often longer-term, over time.
The researcher (or/and their assistants) selects the methods and the questions, asks the questions, interprets and analyzes the data, draws conclusions, makes recommendations and writes the report.	The facilitator involves and works with the co-researchers to choose the methods and the questions to be asked (and possibly by) the co-researchers, and circulates the responses among them; and decide on new actions, and then experiment with these, self-monitoring them, and so on.
The researcher sees disparities of power as irrelevant, or accepts them as inevitable, works around or avoids them as much as possible.	Disparities of power require the facilitator to design strategies so that all people may both speak and be heard accurately.
The researcher remains at arm's length from each stakeholder, examining the operation of the variables "through a microscope."	The facilitator enters into an engaged, inter-subjective process with the participants, and together they hold up mirrors and magnifying glasses to themselves and each other.
Worst possible results are "getting it wrong" and being rejected as "academic" or vilified as "subjective" or "political" (or worse, you don't even know the impact) or you leave behind simmering resentment from those who never felt heard.	Worst possible results are that self-understandings are still not achieved and the group or organization is left with the status-quo practices and conflicts. (Facilitator vilified for not having come up with the answers).
Best possible results are you get it right are lauded as "objective," although it may either not be different from what was thought, expected or planned at the outset, or it may have been used to introduce changes wanted only by one or some parties (who had the power to make them).	Best possible results are new insights are gained by all the relevant players and are more or less quickly applied in practice without the need for executive direction. (But it never gets written up!) Over a sequence of cycles, more and more desirable changes are the result of the inquiry.

Source: Wadsworth 2006: 333.

Yoland Wadsworth sees the role of researcher in PAR closer to that of a facilitator. Wadsworth (1998) views PAR as a new paradigm of science. Whereas the traditional positivist sees the world as having a single reality that can be known by an independent, neutral and objective scientist using the scientific method and controlled experiments, PAR researchers rely on an interpretivist approach, which focuses on the meaning people assign to reality.

Models of PAR

Many scholars have developed models of PAR. The one suggested by Sara Kindon, Rachel Pain and Mike Kesby clearly demonstrates the relationship between action and reflection (see Table 6-2).

Another useful model was developed by James Dudley. In it, he demonstrates how participants are involved at each stage of the research process (see Table 6-3). Dudley views PAR as a way of protecting participants, encouraging their involvement and providing control over how the results will be utilized.

Participatory action research (PAR) was used in a study with members of a mental health consumer-run organization. The researchers involved felt this was a good match because consumer-run organizations, such as consumer-

Table 6-2 Kindon-Pain-Kesby Model of PAR

Reflection	On research design, ethics, power relations, knowledge construction process, representation and accountability.
Action	Build relationships Identify roles, responsibilities and ethics procedures. Establish a memorandum of understanding. Collaboratively design research process and tools. Discuss and identify desired action outcomes.
Reflection	On research questions, design, working relationships and information requirements.
Action	Work together to implement research process and undertake data collection. Enable participation of others. Collaboratively analyze information generated. Begin planning action together.
Reflection	On research processes. Evaluate participation and representation of others. Assess need for further research and/or various action options.
Action	Plan research-informed action, which may include feedback to participants and influential others.
Reflection	Evaluate action and process as a whole.
Action	Identify options for further participatory research and action with or without academic researchers.

Source: Kindon, Pain and Kesby 2007: 15.

Table 6-3 Model of PAR

Stages in the Research Process	Implementation
Understand the research topic	Involve all research partners in offering their views about the research problem and its causes. Ask those affected by the problem to clearly articulate the problem, its scope and all of the research partners.
Focus on the research question	Involve all research partners in deciding on the research question and the purpose of the change the research is designed to accomplish.
Design the study	Select a collaborative research team of professional and lay researchers to create the research design. Train lay researchers to participate in the research design.
Collect the data	Train lay researchers to assist in data collection.
Analyze the data	Train lay researchers to assist in data analysis.
Prepare the report	Report findings in accessible formats to all stakeholder groups.

Source: James Dudley 2010: 32.

survivor initiatives (CSIs), share common PAR values of empowerment, support and social change. In this study, the PAR approach was characterized by the following: (a) the involvement of CSI members in developing the study proposal and in selecting the study sites; (b) the hiring, training and supporting of consumers as co-researchers; (c) the use of a steering committee which met bi-monthly to guide all aspects of the study (including representatives from each of the participating CSIs, the Ontario Peer Development Initiative—the provincial umbrella group of CSIs — and the researchers); and (d) ongoing feedback and dissemination of study findings in both popular (e.g., news bulletins, forums) and professional (e.g., journal articles) formats. (Nelson et al. 2008: 194)

Degrees of Citizen Participation

Research involves a range of citizen participation, sometimes calling for maximum involvement in decision-making and participation and at other times, much less. As a way of analyzing the degree of citizen participation, Steven Hick (1997: 68) proposes a two dimensional grid, with one dimension locating the degree to which citizens are involved in the research (either directly or indirectly), and the other identifying the degree to which citizens are involved in conducting the research (either actively or passively) (see Figure 6-2). According to Hick, Quadrant A represents research projects involving maximum citizen control and involvement, while those with the least

Figure 6-2

Quadrant A Direct/Active	Quadrant B Direct/Passive
Quadrant C Indirect/Active	Quadrant D Indirect/Passive

amount of citizen control and involvement would be located in Quadrant D. In the ideal participatory approach, Quadrant A, citizens would control all major decisions, such as choosing the research question, deciding on the methodology, carrying out the data collection and analysis, preparing the research report and, finally, deciding how to use the results of the research. At the other extreme, those projects located in Quadrant D, citizen involvement is limited to answering questions chosen by the researchers and would not be considered PAR. The indirect/passive combination captures the great majority of traditional research projects, in which citizens are objects of the research and their knowledge is used to answer research questions chosen by the researcher.

Forming Equitable Relationships in PAR

As we have said, one of the core values of PAR is active involvement of users and other interested groups in the research process. As in structural social work practice, it is important to consider power differentials and the experience of marginalized groups being denied access to power. It is thus necessary to make efforts to neutralize this and form truly equitable relationships. The following questions come from an example of PAR on cultural competence, which refers to an ability and willingness to work effectively with people from a variety of cultures (Shiu-Thorton 2003: 1362–63).

1. Conducting a cultural self-assessment:
   - Is there willingness for researchers and funders to identify their own socially and culturally constructed perspectives and methods for performing research?
   - Are researchers and funders willing to identify the ways in which their own professional socialization to performing research may facilitate or be a barrier to performing PAR?
   - Is there a commitment by research professionals to be fully aware and mindful of their own cultural beliefs, values and behaviours?
   - Are researchers committed to identifying activities and establishing time to engage in self-reflected assessment?
   - Will funders support it?
2. Understanding the dynamics of difference:
   - How deeply do researchers understand the historical, social, po-

litical and cultural context of the communities where research is conducted?
- How are the different partnership roles described, understood, and respected?
- What is communication like between community partners? Researchers, including researchers of colour? Project staff? Community partners and researchers, including researchers of colour? Community partners, researchers and project staff?
- What is communication like between all partners and the funder?
- How are different perspectives expressed and disagreements resolved?
- Who has power? Is power shared? How?

3. Adapting to diversity:
- Who sets the agenda?
- Who establishes the timeline?
- Who interprets the results?
- How are findings shared?
- What is the role of funders in supporting culturally competent research?
- How are relationships sustained beyond the funding period?

A Participatory Evaluation of the Banking Accessibility Pilot Project

This example of PAR, mentioned previously in this chapter, involved maximum citizen participation. It was conducted by two Carleton University MSW students. This evaluation of the Banking Accessibility Pilot Project (BAPP) involved four participants of BAPP, the two students and a retired social work faculty member, who acted as a project facilitator. The BAPP evaluation team was responsible for the research design, data collection, data analysis and reporting of results. The evaluation team was supported and guided by an advisory team consisting of BAPP participants, social workers, relatives of the participants and bank representatives. The advisory team had been in place since the beginning of the pilot project.

BAPP was launched November 8, 2007, by the Canadian Mental Health Association (CMHA) Ottawa Branch in partnership with the TD Canada Trust bank. BAPP had thirty participants. Its objectives were to help people living with serious mental illness gain access to bank accounts and to set up services tailored to their individual needs. The services offered included no-fee banking, automatic deposits from work income and/or government payments, automatic payment of bills at no charge and helping participants develop banking strategies and awareness of other bank services. The overall goal of BAPP was to have participants be financially independent and confident in their ability to manage money. A broader objective was to provide a model for other banks/TD Canada Trust branches, as this was the first such project in Canada.

The research project began with the launch of the BAPP program in November 2007, and the data collection ended by December 31, 2008. The evaluation team met weekly until February 2009. The project design included a brief one-time interview for the participants of BAPP and their family members and focus groups with social workers of the participants and bank employees. Where in-person data collection was not possible, phone interviews were conducted at the CMHA office. The participants of the evaluation were audio-taped (with their permission). The data analysis compared these results with those from a start-up interview, administered to BAPP participants at the beginning of the project. The team also analyzed responses to open-ended questions, using qualitative data analysis techniques. The results were reported via an evaluation report and through presentations to research partner groups, including project participants, social workers and other banks/TD Canada Trust branches.

Ethical Issues

The participants in the study were persons living with mental health issues, their social workers/case managers, parents or guardians, and selected members of bank staff. Accordingly, the physical and psycho-social wellbeing of all persons living with mental health issues were of primary concern. If a BAPP participant indicated need for a particular accommodation, the BAPP team made every attempt to satisfy the request. For example, one participatory evaluator was "not a morning person"; as a result, regular meetings were scheduled for after 1 p.m. Another participant evaluator preferred not to meet at night; meetings were concluded prior to sundown.

Four service users who acted as participatory evaluators were involved at every stage in the evaluation process. This helped to assure that the BAPP evaluation team engaged with participants in a manner that was non-intrusive and respectful. Moreover, the interview and focus group questions were in large part constructed by the evaluation team. The questions were easily understood and framed in a non-threatening and neutral manner. For those who were unable to read, the evaluation team was instructed to read the contents slowly upon request. In case participants did not at first understand what was being asked of them, the evaluation team members were trained to ask interview questions in a variety of ways. If participant evaluators required assistance at any point, student researchers or the project evaluator were available on site. Social workers/case managers also agreed to make themselves accessible in the event that their participating clients required support.

In terms of collecting private and sensitive information, participants were identified by a number, and the project evaluator was the only person who had a record of these. The list was stored in a locked box, separate from the data collected in interviews and focus groups. Participants were informed of this procedure and were also notified that the information they provided would only be seen by members of the BAPP evaluation team. For this reason, all members of the evaluation team signed CMHA confidentiality agreements. The data collected from each participant was aggregated with data collected from all participants. That way, the information presented by individual participants could not be identified. All participants were provided with a summary of the evaluation findings and had access to the full report, if they wished. An oral presentation of the findings was made as well, and participants were invited to attend.

The research team reported the following results:

> The pilot project has achieved success far beyond its initial goals. It has been a win-win for both the participants and support workers. The benefits also extend to bank staff who feel good about extending hospitable banking to people who might have been, or felt themselves to be, excluded from mainstream banking.
>
> The benefits to caregiving family members were another added bonus. This banking service can offer relief from potentially unhealthy dependency relationships between parents and adult children with serious mental illness who cannot effectively manage their own finances yet whose situation is not so serious as to require the use of a public trustee. It also presents the hope of providing long-term financial management and related security as these parent caregivers grow old.[1]

DISCUSSION QUESTIONS

1. Describe the advantages and disadvantages of PAR.
2. What do you think might make you uncomfortable with sharing power with respect to important research decisions?
3. Are there situations when you would veto decisions made by research participants? Explain.
4. If you found yourself in a situation where the advisory committee made a decision which you believe went against basic research ethics, would you be comfortable speaking up? Explain.

Note

1. From the research report of Hadas Elkayam, Lindsay Snow, Bessa Whitmore and the Canadian Mental Health Association 2008.

7. Research with Aboriginal People

Aboriginal people perceive that they are one of the most studied populations on earth (Wilson 2008). Citing the Royal Commission on Aboriginal People, Marilyn Bennett states that Aboriginal people believe they have been "researched to death" and will no longer tolerate colonial intrusion by researchers (2004: 20). Most of this "white research" was conducted by western-trained researchers who operated within the western positivist and empiricist paradigm (Smith 1999). Bennett states: "Research findings are often cloaked in academic jargon, are often unintelligible to communities and have largely been irrelevant to community needs" (19). She adds that "academic reputations, so the argument goes, have been built on the backs of Aboriginal subjects and at the political and economic expense of Aboriginal Communities" (19). While these researchers may have believed that their efforts would contribute to the greater good of the people they studied, they nevertheless imposed a western cultural perspective on populations whose values, traditions and worldview differ entirely.

So why are we, as non-Aboriginal researchers, encouraging social work students to carry out research with First Nations communities and organizations? While all research done for Aboriginal communities and organizations should ideally be carried out by trained Aboriginal researchers, the reality is that the demand for research far outstrips the supply. For the time being, non-Aboriginal researchers will continue to be called on to carry out research for these organizations. As Bennett states: "Aboriginal leaders clearly recognize that the information needs of their communities are obvious, but they denounce the monopolistic control of academia over the research process" (19).

Every so often, we receive requests from Aboriginal organizations in Ottawa to conduct research. For example, a few years ago, the First Nations Child and Family Caring Society of Canada asked us to conduct a formative program evaluation on the impact of a conference on reconciliation on conference participants. More recently, the Wabano Centre for Aboriginal Health requested a needs assessment on urban Aboriginal families who had been involved with child protection agencies. Both projects were carried out by student teams that included at least one First Nations social work student.

The following abstract describes the research on the Wabano Centre for Aboriginal Health:

The national capital is currently undergoing significant demographic changes, many of which will shape the way social work will be practised in the future. As urban migration of Aboriginal peoples continues at a steady rate, social workers will continue to face added challenges. Ottawa has one of the fastest rising urban Aboriginal populations in the country and the largest number of Inuit people living outside of the North. There is a growing concern among service providers that the child welfare system has put Aboriginal focused interventions as second to their own. This has resulted in an interlocking issue: an overrepresentation of First Nations, Inuit and Métis children in the system and increasing reliance on Aboriginal agencies to shoulder the responsibility of the effects that overrepresentation has caused with minimal staffing, token collaboration and overwhelming fiscal restraints. Effective social work practice in the future has two options: keep structural change on the forefront by using empowerment and personal commitment to change or comply with the usual regulatory bodies such as the child welfare system and continue to work separately. MSW students from Carleton University document the outcomes from the project: Needs Assessment of Urban Aboriginal Families Involved with the Child Welfare System," which looks at client access of services in an urban Aboriginal health centre in Ottawa... service gaps experienced by the clients of the centre [need to be filled] and... the working constraints experienced by the operational staff [need to be modified] in anticipation of changing the role of social workers to include liaison skills within the urban Aboriginal health centre setting.[1]

Social work practice with Aboriginal peoples has, historically, also operated from a western positivist paradigm. In her review of this social work practice, Raven Sinclair, an Aboriginal social work scholar, states: "The social work profession and social work education have not been free from colonial influence. The colonialistic actions and attitudes towards Aboriginal people have been deliberate and calculated; designed to displace and distance the people from their land and resources" (2004: 50). Government policy, supported by the views of many Canadians, aimed to assimilate Aboriginal people into western culture as quickly as could be managed.

We now acknowledge this as wrong. We recognize the damage done by such initiatives as the "sixties scoop," when thousands of First Nations children were forcibly removed from their families by white social workers and placed in non-Aboriginal foster and adoptive homes far from their communities (Johnston 1983). According to Sinclair, "it is often stated that the intentions of social workers who went to reserves and apprehended children were good, albeit misguided" (50). More recently, efforts are often made to place Aboriginal children in need of protection with members of their extended families or at least in their own communities (Menzies and van de Sande 2003). In B.C., many First Nations are taking complete responsibility for child welfare (Strega and Aski-Esquao 2009). In spite of these changes, a disproportionate number of Aboriginal children still end up in the child welfare system (Blackstock 2009).

What lessons are to be learned from this history? While we cannot undo the damage of the past, we need to do everything possible to support the self-determination of Aboriginal people. To start, we should encourage efforts to develop schools of social work for Aboriginal students taught by Aboriginal faculty who operate from an Aboriginal cultural and theoretical paradigm. Sinclair argues: "Aboriginal social work education is held to support the assertion that a decolonizing pedagogy is a contemporary cultural imperative; that culturally appropriate and sociologically relevant teaching and healing models must evolve and translate into practice and service delivery that will meet the needs of future generations" (49). A few such programs already exist, for example, the School of Indian Social Work at the First Nations University of Canada, the Nicola Valley Institute of Technology in British Columbia and the Native Human Services Program at Laurentian University in Sudbury, Ontario.

We should also support the work of First Nations scholars to develop an Aboriginal research paradigm. Shawn Wilson, in his book on the development of an Indigenous research paradigm, says:

> My goal in doing this work is to help other Indigenous scholars by beginning to articulate an Indigenous research paradigm. I sincerely hope that it will help to substantiate the Indigenous research done by others, so that there will be one less hurdle for them to jump. (2008: 127; see also Smith 1999)

Social Workers and Aboriginal People

For non-Aboriginal social workers, it is important to know and understand the history of colonialism and western, white hegemony, which has characterized social work practices with Aboriginal people. Active involvement of professional social workers in First Nations communities began relatively recently and dramatically intensified during the 1960s, the period referred to as the "sixties scoop" (Johnston 1983). At the time, social workers were almost exclusively Euro-Canadians trained in southern Canadian cities with little or no knowledge of Aboriginal culture other than that which they learned on the job or independently. They applied standards relevant to white Canadian, often urban-centred, culture to Aboriginal people, often living in Northern rural communities. If social workers believed that an Aboriginal child was in need of protection, they would apprehend the child and arrange for placement in a foster or adoptive home, usually with a "white" family living far away from the child's home community.

During this period, very little was written about social work practice with First Nations people. The first mention in a major publication appeared in 1978, in the report by the Canadian Council on Children and Youth entitled *Admittance Restricted*. This report was the first to outline the extent of the over-representation of Native children in child welfare services. The report quotes Douglas Sanders, one of its authors:

> The differences between the material standards of whites and Indians and the differences between the child-rearing practices of the two groups has resulted in excessive apprehension of Indian children. (133)

This situation led the authors of the report to conclude:

> The ideal, of course would be a comprehensive child welfare programme in every community, staffed by skilled native workers, controlled by the community and operating in accordance with its culture and needs. Only in such a system would Native communities have a chance of achieving what the Inuit communities have managed to maintain to a greater extent — self-sufficiency in child welfare. Unfortunately, to judge from present circumstances, it may well be some time before this ideal is reached. (135)

It seems these authors anticipated what is now regarded by many social work authors as the only resolution of community needs.

In 1980, Philip Hepworth, on behalf of the Canadian Council on Social Development, conducted a comprehensive study of foster care and adoption in Canada. He provided a detailed description of the extent to which Aboriginal children were over-represented in child welfare services in each province. For instance, Hepworth stated that, in 1977, 20 percent of all children in care were Aboriginal. The study is one of the most widely quoted references on the subject of Canadian child welfare.

Research conducted by Patrick Johnston in 1983, entitled *Native Children and the Child Welfare System*, had an even greater impact on Aboriginal child welfare and has often been referred to in support of First Nations' control over their own child welfare system. Drawing on census data from the provincial ministries responsible for child welfare, the author points out that by the 1970s, Aboriginal children were 4.5 times more likely than non-Aboriginal children to be in the care of child welfare system. This situation led Edwin

79

Kimmelman, Associate Chief Judge of the Manitoba Family Court, to describe the situation in 1985 as systematic "cultural genocide' (Comeau and Santin 1995: 141).

Studies such as the ones conducted by Hepworth and Johnston have led social work authors in Canada to engage in some soul searching to find explanations for the existence of the crisis in Aboriginal child welfare. Brad McKenzie and Pete Hudson (1985) offer three sets of theoretical explanations of why child welfare workers take assimilationist stances. The first suggests that workers rely heavily on psycho-social theories of human development and interpret child neglect as the result of individual deviation. The second explanation posits that workers acknowledge the cultural differences between Aboriginal and non-Aboriginal people and regard social problems as stemming from the difficulty Aboriginal families have in adjusting to mainstream society. The solution lies, essentially, in helping Aboriginal people to assimilate into white, mainstream culture. In the third theoretical explanation, workers believe that the problems found in Aboriginal child welfare are the result of a socio-economic structure that creates poverty and despair for Aboriginal people, leaving them with a sense of powerlessness. Regardless of which of the three explanations is used by workers, an assimilationist orientation is the result. McKenzie and Hudson suggest that a thorough understanding of the situation can only be achieved if one goes beyond this level of explanation to examine the basic relationship between the two cultures:

> Using this analytical framework, consideration of the dominant society's access to power and resources which can be utilized in overcoming resistance and subjugating an indigenous society becomes important. A conflict perspective of race relations leads to an examination of colonialism.... This view provides a more complete understanding of the current failures in the Native child welfare field and leads to an examination of needed changes in institutional policies and practices in the development of responses oriented to the objective of decolonization. (129)

An Aboriginal Research Paradigm

The development of a uniquely Aboriginal research paradigm has taken place thanks to the efforts of a few Aboriginal scholars who have overcome significant barriers imposed by a western positivist and empiricist academic culture. Citing the work of Patsy Steinhauer, Shawn Wilson (2008) describes four phases in this development. The first phase, which occurred roughly in the 1960s and early 1970s, saw most Aboriginal scholars working within a positivist framework. To be accepted by western universities, they attempted to be western scholars. During the second phase, which took place in the

1980s and early 1990s, Aboriginal scholars began to question and challenge the appropriateness of imposing a western scientific paradigm, but continued doing so to avoid academic marginalization. Lauri Gilchrist points out that volumes of research have generated a great deal of data on Aboriginal people, but "there is little research which Aboriginal peoples have been able to determine themselves" (1999: 70). The third phase, during the later part of the 1990s, can be characterized as a period of decolonization. A good example of work done during this phase is the book by Linda Tuhiwai Smith (1999) entitled *Decolonizing Methodologies*. The fourth and current phase sees Aboriginal scholars working from a specifically Aboriginal research perspective, finally being accepted by mainstream academic institutions. As Wilson points out, there is now an ever-increasing number of Aboriginal students completing their PhDs.

Wilson conceptualizes an Indigenous research paradigm as a circle of four parts, similar to the medicine wheel (see Figure 7-1). The four parts, which are not separate but blend from one into the next to form a whole, include "axiology, ontology, epistemology and methodology" (2008: 70).

Axiology refers to the study of nature, ontology deals with the nature of reality, epistemology is the study of knowledge, and methodology has to do with the procedures or logic used to answer questions. These terms all relate to the methods used to arrive at an understanding of reality. However, as Wilson explains, an Indigenous research paradigm recognizes that there are multiple realities or truths. What is important is not determining which external truth or reality one should adopt, but the relationship one has with reality. Therefore, an Indigenous research paradigm would have us focus more on the relationships between things and people and less on the things. Aboriginal researchers focus on the connections between people, themselves and the land, and not on individual people or objects. For researchers who

Figure 7-1 Indigenous Research Paradigm

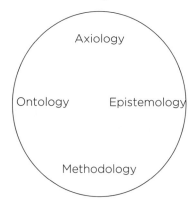

Axiology

Ontology   Epistemology

Methodology

follow an Indigenous paradigm, concepts such as reliability, validity and statistical significance lose their meaning. Unlike the beliefs of researchers who function within a western scientific paradigm, those who operate from an Indigenous research paradigm recognize that they are not neutral and objective observers.

As well, Aboriginal researchers understand that there is a relationship between themselves and their research and between themselves and the community where they work. They appreciate that their research must result in building respectful relationships and that they are accountable to the community they are serving (Wilson 2008). This is in sharp contrast to the western mainstream paradigm, which sees the researcher as a separate, autonomous individual free from the influences of society.

The OCAP Principles

What principles should guide the research of non-Aboriginal researchers who are asked to conduct research for Aboriginal communities or organizations? Aboriginal communities and organizations will no longer permit non-Aboriginal researchers to come in at will, collect their data and leave. More and more Aboriginal organizations have adopted the OCAP principles, which refer to ownership, control, access and possession.[2] These principles have been adopted to ensure the self-determination of First Nations and the preservation and development of their culture. They allow First Nations organizations and communities to make decisions on how, why, when, where and by whom the research is conducted.

Ownership
This principle refers to the relationship First Nations People have with their cultural knowledge. It states that an organization or community owns the data collected and the information resulting from the research conducted for their organization or community.

Control
The principle of control affirms that First Nations communities and organizations have the right to control all aspects of the research, from the design and implementation to the dissemination of the results.

Access
First Nations must have access to all data and information about themselves and their communities regardless of where the information is stored. Furthermore, First Nations have the right to decide who else has access to the data and information. Permission on access should only be granted through formal protocols.

Possession

Possession is closely related to ownership but refers to the physical control of the data and information. This principle requires that a mechanism be developed for the ownership and control of data and information.

Some of the OCAP principles are exemplified in the following research project carried out by Carleton University students. In the following quote, a student researcher describes her thoughts as she prepares to conduct interviews as part of a community-based research project in partnership with an Aboriginal organization:

> As a white woman preparing to conduct interviews in an Aboriginal organization, I had to touch base with myself, and my ability to present myself as an interested ally, rather than an academic expert. I am very passionate about what XXXX does as an organization, and as a result, have studied the colonial/patriarchal framework of Aboriginal people.... One of my biggest challenges as a researcher for this organization was to determine to what end that passion was useful, and to what end it could be perceived as academic know-it-all fervor.[3]

Another student talks about her experience of the meeting where the research group consults with participants about the research instrument and she hears their concerns about research information getting back to their community:

> We had forwarded a letter of information and consent to the potential participants with the project description, issues of confidentiality and ambiguity, and the risks and benefits of participating in our research project. We all introduced ourselves and went over the project. The participants looked over their letters of information and had many insightful questions. They expressed some concern with how to protect themselves and the people they were talking about. They were concerned that the information, if written in a specific way, would allow the people they had spoken about to be able to recognize themselves and the potential impact this could have in their future success with connecting and speaking to other families in similar situations.[4]

Participatory Action Research with Aboriginal Organizations

One method that seems most conducive in respecting the OCAP principles is PAR. The principles of PAR, described in the previous chapter, lend themselves to ensuring the self-determination of First Nations. To briefly review some of these principles, PAR requires that the problem definition originates from the community, that the beneficiary is the community and not the researcher, and that the community is a full partner and involved in all aspects of the research. Bennett explains: "With the help of PAR, a healing process began that was initiated by Aboriginal Peoples, and with the determination that their own knowledge would never again be overridden by outside expertise" (2004: 22).

Interest in participatory approaches to research by Aboriginal groups began after the publication the so-called "White Paper" in 1969. This document, prepared by Jean Chrétien, Minister of Indian Affairs under the Trudeau government, called for the abolition of the *Indian Act* and the assimilation of First Nations people into mainstream Canadian society. Ted Jackson explains:

> It is not surprising that strong interest in Aboriginal-defined and Aboriginal-controlled research approaches coincided with the politicization of Aboriginal organizations in response to the federal government's assimilationist white paper of 1969. Aboriginal leaders began to see that research activities could assist in the movement toward political strength and, ultimately, political self-determination. (1993: 49)

Arguably the most ambitions example of participatory research conducted by Aboriginal people was the Royal Commission on Aboriginal People (RCAP). The extensive study was entirely under the control of First Nations representatives. RCAP was formed after the failed Meech Lake Accord and the Oka crisis, which took place north of Montreal in 1990. Members of the Commission travelled extensively across the country visiting many First Nations communities and interviewing countless groups and individuals. The RCAP report, published in 1996, was over 4,000 pages in length and included over 400 recommendations.[5]

A project conducted by Carleton University MSW students on a program called Missing Sisters illustrates the principles of OCAP and PAR. These students set the following guidelines for themselves in conducting this research:

> As researchers working with Aboriginal people, our research team will be very cognizant of the following considerations:
>
> - Project must strive to adhere to Aboriginal principles when applicable.
> - Due to colonization and subsequent trauma(s), historically Aboriginals have been designated as "subjects" within research.
> - This research project will hold participants as active and valued partners in the creation of knowledge.
> - Project will strive to capture participants as Aboriginal voices and authentic knowledge keepers.
> - As researchers, the literature review, other research docu-

ments and activities will focus in part on expanding the research team's Aboriginal cultural knowledge base, Aboriginal worldview and ways of being.[6]

The following is the abstract of their research:

Missing Sisters: Story Telling as Medicine" is a qualitative study which examines the experiences and knowledge gained by participants who work within the Sisters in Spirit (SIS) Initiative. The Initiative was created to bring awareness of the disproportionate number of Aboriginal women who have gone missing or have been murdered in Canada. The aim of the SIS Initiative is to address not only some of the gaps in knowledge, but also formulating an appropriate cultural response in relation to Aboriginal peoples. We interviewed six participants who are staff members of the SIS Initiative to explore their experiences of working with these families. This is consistent with the conference themes of Violence in the Family, and Human Rights, Advocacy and Social Justice, because the participants bear witness to the minimal supports for families of missing or murdered Aboriginal women. The study focused on capturing the tacit knowledge and felt experiences of the participants, as the information could be lost, much like these missing and murdered women, if and when the participants of the SIS Initiative move on to other work.

According to the Native Women's Association of Canada (NWAC), "as of March 31, 2009, 520 cases of missing or murdered Aboriginal women and girls had been entered into the NWAC database" (2009, p. 88). The SIS initiative was created in response to this phenomenon, which many argue (Amnesty International, 2004; Bourassa, Hampton and Kubik, 2009; MacDonald, 2005) is directly linked to the colonization of Aboriginal people in Canada.

Our research findings will assist practitioners in learning to work with Aboriginal families who have lost loved ones. It also documents the personal and professional challenges that are inevitably faced by those working on the "front lines" with families who have experienced significant trauma. Through the use of Aboriginal perspective, the project has captured Aboriginal voices of the participants as authentic knowledge keepers.

DISCUSSION QUESTIONS

1. If you are a non-Aboriginal researcher, what are some of the challenges you would face in conducting research with Aboriginal people?
2. How would you address the resistance Aboriginal people may manifest in working with you?
3. Do you believe the positivist approach is appropriate in conducting research with Aboriginal people? Explain.
4. In what way would you ensure that traditional knowledge is incorporated in your research?

Notes

1. Pam Parent, Rashida Collins, Melissa Chung, Kristy Fearon, student research project, Carleton University, 2009.
2. See for example, "First Nations Principles of OCAP" at <http://www.rhs-ers.ca/english/ocap.asp>.
3. Meredith Coffin, Reflexive journal , February 2010
4. Jennifer Derraugh, Reflexive journal, February 2010
5. <http://www.ainc-inac.gc.ca/ap/rrc-eng.asp>.
6. Meredith Coffin, Jennifer Derraugh, Gail Toups and Julie Westwood, Missing Sisters student research project, Carleton University, 2010.

8. Program Evaluations

Program evaluation is likely the most common type of research carried out by social service organizations. As mentioned, for several years, the School of Social Work at Carleton University has offered a graduate course on research where students conduct research projects for service organizations in Ottawa. Most of the requests for research we receive are for program evaluations. Unfortunately, few organizations have the resources to carry out their own evaluations and are often obliged to turn to outside research consultants for help.

We have also stated that we advocate using a structural approach to social work research. To reiterate, coming from a structural perspective implies that the research we conduct, whether quantitative or qualitative, will be informed by anti-oppressive principles and lead to structural changes. With respect to program evaluations, this means that clients served by the program being evaluated should be involved in the research to the greatest extent possible. The most effective way of ensuring their involvement is to create an advisory committee that includes both client and staff representatives, with clients having at least an equal say in research-related decisions.

This chapter outlines several common reasons for conducting program evaluations and two common forms of program evaluations: formative and summative. We also describe several research designs, including the logic model, which offers a simple and practical approach to evaluations.

Reasons for Conducting Program Evaluations

Carl Brun (2005), in his text *A Practical Guide to Social Service Evaluation,* provides a list of the most common reasons why social service organizations do program evaluations. First on the list is that many organizations require evaluations as a condition for meeting the standards set by their accrediting body. As stated by Brun, most social work agencies are accredited and must undergo regular reviews. The type of requests we have received supports this view. An administrator of one of our local agencies admitted to us that they had recently lost their accreditation. He was hoping to use the results of a program evaluation to reverse that decision. Fortunately, the results of the evaluation were generally positive and the agency was reinstated.

The next most common reason on Brun's list is that funding bodies, whether governmental or private, require program evaluations as a condition of receiving funds. In fact, it is rare today that funding would be offered without a stipulation requiring an evaluation. Funders need to know that money is being used effectively. For example, a group of students ran focus groups to gain information regarding a program providing reproductive and sexual health information to Muslim youth. The funder had mandated this evaluation as a condition of the funding.

Another reason for evaluations is that members of boards of directors request this information. They may have concerns about certain programs or they may simply feel the need to demonstrate the effectiveness of programs. The same applies to administrators and supervisors, who may have questions about some of their programs or the performance of their staff. Staff members themselves may be interested in evaluating the programs they run as a way of identifying areas that need improvement. Finally, collaborating agencies may request an evaluation of programs to which they refer clients.

Quite far down the list of reasons provided by Brun, unfortunately, is that service users request a program evaluation. In our view, accountability to service users should be at the top of the list; however, few clients feel they have the right to hold organizations accountable. They may feel that the service they receive is a privilege and not a right and that if they complain, services will be withheld. It is for this reason that research ethics boards insist that client input in evaluation research be kept strictly confidential.

The client's reluctance to speak up is another important reason for creating an advisory body where client and organizational representatives have parity. Clients need to receive a clear message from researchers that they have at least as much say as organization representatives in choosing the focus of the research. As you can begin to appreciate, program evaluations can be a political minefield. As Dudley (2010) explains, ideally, the various partners are able to discuss their respective agendas in an open and proactive manner in order to achieve the ultimate goal of contributing to the enhancement of the program.

Formative Program Evaluations

Generally speaking, there are two types of program evaluations, formative and summative (Rubin and Babbie 2008; Royse 2008; Marlow 2005). As the name suggests, formative evaluations are used with programs that are still at the formative stage of development. This type of evaluation is not concerned with program outcomes but looks instead at the planning and implementation of the program. It potentially relies on a variety of designs and approaches. Input is sought from clients and staff and occasionally from community representatives. The results of the formative evaluation are used by program planners to make modifications to the program as needed. A formative evaluation attempts to answer the question: "What would make this a better program?" (Royse 2008: 299).

Royse (2008) describes a number of possible ways to conduct a formative evaluation. One way is to obtain expert consultation. An organization which has enough program development money might retain a recognized expert in the field to conduct a review of the program. This expert could be an academic, a consultant or an experienced practitioner who has a recognized expertise in the area of program reviews. Depending on the scope of the review, this person may want to visit the facilities, examine program documents and interview staff and clients. They might notice possible problems not immediately obvious to program planners, such as the lack of adequate office space or equipment for staff, a public area that is not inclusive to certain cultural groups or a location that is not accessible to target client populations. The consultant's report usually includes a list of recommended changes that the organizations could make to improve the program.

If there is no money for an outside expert, the second method proposed by Royse (2008) is the use of "model standards." An organization could locate a set of standards used by similar organizations (e.g., through a literature or internet search) that describe the necessary elements for a program to be of high quality. For instance, a family service agency may decide to consult the standards established by Family Services Canada.[1]

The third option would be for the organization to form an ad hoc review committee, which could be made up of clients, staff, board members and community representatives. The task of this committee would be to design and conduct an internal formative evaluation. The committee would need to decide on the focus of the research, the methods to be used and who to invite to participate. If committee members are unsure about the best approach, they could call on a representative from a local university or other expert who may be willing to act as an (unpaid) advisor.

Research Designs

Program evaluation, like other forms of research generally follow three kinds of research designs, each of which serves a different purpose. The first is exploratory design, used when little is known about a given topic (Royse 2008). If a new area of interest emerges for which there is little or no previous research, an exploratory design can be used to fill the initial gap. A good example from the past would be abuse against women by their male partners. Not long ago this was considered a private family matter and not a topic of interest for researchers. An exploratory design would involve asking survivors of abuse as well as practitioners open-ended questions. Initial exploratory studies can help pave the way for further research in the subject area.

The next type is descriptive design, used primarily to describe a population of interest (Royse 2008). A familiar example would be political polls, which describe the voting preferences of the public. An example more related to social work would be in the area of homelessness. An organization interested in serving the homeless may need to describe the nature and extent of homelessness in a given community as part of a request for funding. Information could be gathered from local shelters and soup kitchens. The design describes a certain phenomenon and can provide useful information for establishing and developing new social programs (Marlow 2005).

Third, explanatory design is the kind that has been favoured by traditional researchers. Mainstream science is not only interested in a phenomenon but also the relationship between its events. The explanatory design is popular with scientists because it attempts to identify cause-and-effect relationships. In mainstream research, there are two types of variables, independent, or causal, variables and dependent, or outcome, variables.

In order to establish that a program caused improvement for clients, certain conditions must be met. Dudley (2010: 203) states that there are three such conditions:

1. the intervention *precedes* improvement in the client's goal;
2. the client's goal *improves* significantly after the intervention is implemented; and
3. the intervention is found to be at least partially *responsible* for this improvement, after controlling for possible alternative influences.

An example of an explanatory study would be a program evaluation of a group counselling program to help women develop more positive self-esteem. An explanatory design would allow us to demonstrate that the program caused improvements in their self-esteem. The independent variable would be the group counselling program and the dependent variable would be improvement in self-esteem. We could demonstrate that it was the program that caused the improvement in self-esteem using a classic experimental design (which we describe below). While all three research designs are used in program evaluations, the only one that will determine if a program is effective is the explanatory design. This is because the explanatory design attempts to establish a link between the program, as the independent or causal variable, and the impact on clients, as the dependent or effect variable.

Summative Program Evaluations

Summative program evaluations, also called "outcome evaluations" (Royse 2008), focus on the effectiveness of a program. Christine Marlow (2005) offers a range of summative program evaluation designs, four of which are

1) the one group post-test only design, 2) the one group pre-test post-test design, 3) the pre-test post-test non-equivalent comparison design and 4) the pre-test post-test control group design. Marlow examines each of these using two criteria, internal validity and external validity. By internal validity, she refers to the extent to which the changes in the *dependent variable* are the result of the introduction of the *independent variable* and not some other factor. In other words, does the independent variable cause the dependent variable to change? Referring to our example of the counselling program described above, we would want to show that the improvement in self-esteem was caused by the program and not something else, such as increased family support. By external validity, Marlow refers to whether the research results are generalizable to a wider population. In other words, would our counselling program be effective for other women who experience low self-esteem? If these two criteria are met, the evaluation will allow the researcher to answer the question: "Is this program effective in terms of helping clients?"

The One Group Post-Test Design
This design is the simplest of the summative program designs. Client functioning is measured at the end of the intervention only, using a standardized instrument specifically designed to measure the phenomenon of interest. For example, a program interested in helping clients raise their self-esteem may use the Rosenberg Self-Esteem Scale (1965). With respect to internal validity, because we don't how clients functioned prior to starting the intervention, we also don't know if clients changed. In terms of external validity, if clients are not randomly selected from the population we cannot generalize to the larger population. The only thing this design will tell us is how clients functioned when they finished the program, which, if this is the only information available, is still helpful.

The One Group Pre-Test Post-Test Design
In this design, client functioning is measured at the start of the intervention and again at the end. In terms of internal validity, we know whether clients changed while attending the program, but we don't know if some outside factor influenced the change. If this type of evaluation showed improved self-esteem in the women in the counselling program, it is possible that support from family and friends contributed to the improvement. We cannot say if it was the program that caused the change. In terms of external validity, if clients have not been randomly selected, we cannot generalize. We are therefore still not able to say if the program is effective.

The Pre-Test Post-Test Comparison Group Design
Also called the "quasi experimental design," client functioning is measured at the start and again at the end of the intervention. The results of these measurements are compared to the measurements of a similar but non-

equivalent group of clients who are also tested at two points in time, but who do not participate in the program. In this case, we know whether clients changed *and* we are able to say if they changed more than a similar group of clients who are not in the program. We could, for instance, have invited other women with similar self-esteem issues to participate in a comparison group. However, because the clients have not been randomly assigned to either the program group or the non-program group, we still cannot say if the groups are completely equivalent. To be equivalent, we need a control group. With respect to external validity, without random selection, we cannot generalize.

The Pre-Test Post-Test Control Group

This last design is also called the "classic experimental design" and is the only one that meets the internal and external validity criteria. In this design, participants are randomly selected from the population of clients and assigned at random to either the program (or experimental) group and the control group. Both groups of clients are tested at two points in time, with the program group being tested before and after the intervention. For an evaluation on our self-esteem program to follow a true classic experimental design, we would need a large pool of possible participants. If there are enough women on a waiting list, we could select women and randomly assign them to either the program or the control group. If the program group improves significantly more than the control group, we are finally able to say that it is the counselling program that caused the change, that clients are being helped by the program and that the results are generalizable to a wider population of clients.

While this last design is considered ideal in terms of summative program evaluations, it is not without its drawbacks. One of the criticisms concerns the "reactive effect" (Marlow 2005) of the pre-test and post-test approach. Having been tested once, clients will be familiar with the testing instrument and will know what questions are being asked. Even the control group usually performs better during the post-test. In our example, we can only hope that the program group will improve much more than the control group. Because of the reactive effect, some researchers skip the pre-test, arguing that if the two groups are equivalent, the post-test will be enough to test the effectiveness of the program.

Another issue raised by Marlow (2005) concerns the ethics involved in establishing a control group. It may be unethical to deny service to clients whose needs may be greater than the ones chosen for the experimental group. For this reason, many organizations opt for a one-group pre- and post-test design even if this means sacrificing "scientific rigour." On the other hand, since many agencies have waiting lists, it may be possible to include some of these people in a control group without causing undue harm.

Program Evaluation Research Steps

Regardless of the type, program evaluations follow steps typical of any research project. The ones suggested by James Dudley (2010: 314) include:

1. understanding the purpose of the agency and the intervention question;
2. involving the partners in a discussion to reach a consensus on the purpose of the research and the research question;
3. designing the study;
4. collecting the data;
5. analyzing the data; and
6. preparing an oral and/or written report and disseminating it.

Most program evaluators see the program evaluation process more narrowly. They identify three broad stages in program development: planning, implementation and outcome, and focus their research only on outcome. Instead, Dudley believes that program evaluation activities should occur at all stages in the development of the program. Dudley (2010: 317) breaks the following three stages down into several steps:

1. *Planning Stage*:
   * document the need for the program;
   * identify the client population;
   * develop a program approach;
   * decide on the qualifications of staff and hire them; and
   * obtain funding.
2. *Implementation Stage*:
   * train staff in delivering the program approach and its technologies;
   * implement the approach;
   * document how the intervention is being implemented;
   * engage clients fully using the intervention; and
   * determine client satisfaction.
3. *Outcome Stage*:
   * measure progress in client outcomes;
   * determine whether the overall program is effective;
   * decide whether to modify the approach or continue it unchanged; and
   * determine how clients who complete the program are different from dropouts.

Client Satisfaction Surveys

One of the more popular forms of program evaluation is the client satisfaction survey. This type of evaluation typically uses a one group post-test only design, testing clients just as they are exiting the program. James Dudley (2009) provides a list of the type of questions that could form the survey. Some examples include: "How satisfied are you with the services that you have been receiving?", "Are you feeling generally satisfied? In what way?" and "What might you be feeling dissatisfied or disappointed about? In what specific possible areas?"

Clients are generally asked to respond to a scale with a range of possible responses (e.g., from strongly agree to strongly disagree). A question such as "How would you rate the service you received?" could be answered with a range of responses such as: excellent, good, average, poor and very poor. This is another area where clients can be helpful in designing evaluations. The survey can be pre-tested using a group of clients to check whether the language is easily understood. Clients can also give input into the design of the survey so it reflects the issues they would also like feedback about.

The difficulty with client satisfaction surveys is that while they do provide useful feedback, they tend to produce artificially positive results. As Bonnie Yegidis et al. (2009), explain, if a questionnaire is mailed to clients, the clients most likely to complete the questionnaire are those who feel positively about the program. They also point out that client satisfaction is not necessarily related to program effectiveness. A client may rate the service as satisfactory because their worker "seemed to care" even if no progress was made on the problem. Yegidis et al. argue that even if clients are questioned about the progress they made, it is almost impossible for satisfaction issues not to influence the results.

Even with these limitations, the client satisfaction surveys may provide valuable feedback. The surveys will likely provide more honest feedback if the questionnaires are anonymous. Also, the most useful surveys tend to use open-ended questions, where clients are free to express their opinions.

One of our students summed up her experience with and opinions about program evaluation this way:

> Maintaining funding for non-profit community organizations is, these days, somewhat of a numbers game that most certainly privileges quantitative methods of data collection and analysis. In reporting to donors it is always nice to include a "success story" or "story of change" but without the "hard data" to show the program has had a positive result on all or most participants, or that it has achieved quantifiable results, there is little hope of sustained funding.[2]

The Logic Model

Another popular tool for conducting program evaluations is the "logic model" (Brun 2005). It is a graphic description of the essential components of a program and how these components are linked to specific objectives and measurable indicators (Rubin and Babbie 2008). While a number of variations exist, the one described by Brun (2005) includes the following five basic components: 1) inputs, 2) goals, 3) strategies, 4) short-term results and 5) long-term results.

Inputs are the sources of information that formed the basis for the development of the program. An example would be the results of an assessment that demonstrated a need for programs to help new immigrants integrate successfully in society. Goals are general statements of the desired outcomes of the intervention program. For example, the goal of a program for new immigrants would be to help immigrants learn to speak English and develop marketable skills. Strategies are the interventions used to reach the goals. In the above example, an agency may organize language and employment training classes. The short-term results are the outcomes which occur immediately after the intervention. In our example, a short-term result would be immigrants learning to speak English and approaching job hunting with self-confidence. Finally, the long-term results are the outcomes that are reached once clients have completed the full program. A long-term result for the above program would be for immigrants to find fulfilling employment and live meaningful lives in their new country. Our example is illustrated in Table 8-1.

The logic model offers a number of benefits for both program planners and front-line social workers. It is useful for planners because it helps organizations conceptualize the components of the program. As Brun (2005) points out, it is impossible to evaluate a program when the goals and strategies are not clearly described with measurable outcomes. The model is also useful for front-line social workers because it helps them clarify the components of their intervention plans. Whether one is planning a major program or an individual intervention, the components of the plan are the same. Social

Table 8-1 The Logic Model

Inputs	New immigrants need help to integrate successfully in society.
Goals	Help immigrants learn to speak English and develop marketable skills.
Strategies	Organize language classes and employment training.
Short-Term Results	Learn to speak English and approach job hunting with self-confidence.
Long-Term Results	Immigrants have successfully found fulfilling employment and are living meaningful lives in their new country.

workers who complete contracts in collaboration with their clients will see the similarities between the logic model and these contracts.

A Research Project with Single Mothers on Social Assistance

The following abstract from a study conducted by Mary Ann Jenkins (2003: 163) is a good example of a formative program evaluation using a qualitative research design:

> In March of 1999, the Ontario government announced a new policy aimed at teen mothers. The 25 million Learning, Earning and Parenting program (LEAP) requires 16- and 17-year old welfare mothers to attend school and take parenting courses. The stated goal of the program is to break the cycle of welfare that traps many young women. In June 2000, the first 23 "graduates" completed the program in Sudbury. To conduct a preliminary evaluation of the program (from the perspective of participants), qualitative semi-structured interviews were conducted with 14 participants of the LEAP program. The results showed how LEAP, a bureaucratic program, which the recipients might have experienced as something quite oppressive, became something more positive and enabling, due to the collaborating of the social workers, the teachers and the students themselves.

Interestingly, Jenkins approached this study from a feminist theoretical perspective, expecting to show how the program had oppressive elements. The young sixteen- and seventeen-year-old female parents were required to attend school as a condition of receiving social assistance benefits. If they did not attend school, benefits would be cut off, meaning they would no longer have the financial means to care for their children. Their cases would then be reported to the local child protection agency and the children would most likely be apprehended and placed in foster care.

We can learn from this study that while we should approach research from a structural and anti-oppressive perspective, we still need listen to our clients with an open mind. None of the women interviewed reported feeling oppressed by the program. Instead, they stated that they found the social work staff and teachers to be very supportive. The young women in the study believed they would not have finished school without the support of the program.

The question remains, however, had Jenkins engaged the young women in a discussion group to help them become conscious of the oppressive elements of the LEAP program, would they have responded as positively? This question, of course, was not within the scope of the study.

DISCUSSION QUESTIONS

1. Have you had experience with program evaluations in the past? Elaborate.
2. What are the pros and cons of involving clients in program evaluations?
3. What would be the difference in program evaluation agendas of program funders versus administrators?
4. What are the ethical issues in using control groups in program evaluations?
5. What are the power issues related to client research partners versus program administrators with respect to program evaluations?

Notes

1. <www.familyservicecanada.org>.
2. Jaime Lenet, Reflexive Journal 1, November 2010.

9. Needs Assessments

After program evaluations, the next most likely type of research requested by social work organizations is a needs assessment. Before organizations can apply for funding for a new program or even to expand on an existing one, they must first justify the extra expense.

There are several reasons for carrying out a needs assessment and different ways to do assessments. As with any community-based research, all interested partners should be involved in conducting a needs assessment. The strength-based approach to conducting a needs assessment is one of the more useful, as it gets us away from focusing on the negative aspects of needs and problems to focusing on the positive aspects of strength and potential. This chapter ends with a case study of research carried out by our MSW students using a strength-based approach to a needs assessment.

A student describes her experience with needs assessments:

> Part of my job at the Adoption Council of Canada (ACC) is to expand the funding base to allow for new programs and services. I have, in turn, written countless funding proposals, to a multitude of corporations, foundations, and government bodies. Looking back, I have asked myself: why are we successful with some proposals? Why are we unsuccessful with others? One of the keys, I believe, is in our use of qualitative research findings. We can report that over 78,000 children and youth are in foster care in Canada; however, it can be the single story of one of those children and youth that can make the difference between a successful and unsuccessful grant submission. The stories give "life" to the numbers. The stories make the numbers "real."[1]

What Are Needs?

James Dudley defines a need "as an aspect to a larger problem identified by a client and perceived to be amenable to change" (2009: 108). He explains that meeting a need is most often the intended focus of a program. However, he cautions against moving too quickly on simply finding out needs, insisting we also look at the underlying causes of the need. For instance, a shelter provides for the immediate needs of homeless people but does not address the underlying causes of homelessness.

Here we enter into ideological and political debates about the responsibility of a society towards its more vulnerable citizens. A neoliberal approach to dealing with homelessness would have society providing only the absolute minimum level of support — or, none at all, given the popularity of the demand that homeless people deal with their addictions or mental health issues before they are allowed into a shelter. Support would include minimal social assistance, homeless shelters and food banks, enough to keep people alive but not much more. On the other hand, a structural approach would see society's responsibility as including social assistance rates that ensure that people have access to decent food, shelter and clothing and are able to fully participate in society. The first step for many people is to secure a decent place to live. This would require policies on full employment, on a minimum wage to provide a decent standard of living and on an adequate supply of low-cost housing.

As social work researchers using a structural perspective, we should therefore do our best to address the underlying causes of social needs. We should not attempt to conduct only research that is politically neutral. Wherever possible, we should use the information gathered from a needs assessment to publicize the causes of problems, lobby local, provincial and federal politicians about the need for policies to address the problems and advocate for real structural changes. As structural social workers, we will also want to ensure that clients or potential clients have maximum input in defining their own needs.

Regardless of ideological or political views, the needs assessment should provide the information required as a basis for program planning. In the previous chapter, we introduced the logic model as a practical approach to program planning and evaluation. Needs assessment results would be the "inputs" to the logic model and are, therefore, essential elements in the program planning process. For example, if an organization is interested in serving homeless people, it must document the nature and extent of their needs. The term "homeless people" is a catch-all phrase which includes not only single adult men but single women, youth, the elderly, people living with mental illness, people with physical and developmental disabilities and families with children. The needs of each of these groups are different. The research should clearly document which group or groups the program intends to help. Also the needs of people living on the street are different from homeless people who are living on the couches of friends and family members. One example of the differing needs of different groups of homeless people can be found at the Ottawa Mission, which provides specialized services for elderly and terminally ill homeless people. The Home Hospice at the Ottawa Mission provides twenty-four-hour palliative care to homeless people facing the final days of their lives so that they do not die alone, in pain, frightened and devoid of dignity. Doctors, nurses, client-care workers and other health care professionals offer hospice patients crucial physical, emotional and spiritual support at every stage of their illness. Patients whose lives are complicated by addictions and mental health issues find a level of care that all people deserve (Ottawa Mission website n.d.).

A needs assessment should also document any existing programs that serve the same population. There may be shelters, food banks, counselling programs, clothing outlets and subsidized housing, all serving the needs of those who are homeless in a given region. All of this information could then be used to develop a program plan or proposal. This plan should outline the type of services to be developed, specific goals and objectives, and where the services will be located. It should also include the possibilities for partnerships with other organizations.

Reasons for Conducting a Needs Assessment

While needs assessments are an essential part of program planning, there are other related reasons for conducting them. Marlow (2005: 72–73) offers the following list:

- determining whether services exist in the community; Marlow suggests using networking skills,[2] the internet and if it exists, a directory of community services;
- determining if there are enough clients; anecdotal information may suggest the need for a given service but there may not be enough potential clients to justify the expense of mounting a new program. There may be another group of clients that could benefit from the services provided (for example, a group of Carleton University MSW students conducted a needs assessment for a local community resource centre showing that there was a large group of new Asian immigrants who could benefit from programs aimed at their needs. The centre did not realize that such a large number of Asian people had moved into the neighbourhood.);
- determining who uses existing services; even if an agency offers a given program, clients may not be accessing the program for a variety of reasons. Clients may not be aware that the program exists or that they are eligible.
- determining what barriers prevent clients from accessing services; even if clients are aware of and eligible for services, they may not be accessing the program for other reasons. Transportation or childcare may be an issue. (A group of Carleton students, for example, explored the barriers faced by Muslim youth to accessing sexual and reproductive health services offered by Planned Parenthood. They found that if the program was given a name that did not refer to sexual health informa-

tion Muslim youth were more likely to participate. The program needed to be called something ambiguous like "Girls Night.") Language may be another barrier. In the Ottawa area, while most organizations offer programs for English and French speaking clients, a growing proportion of the population of Ottawa speaks neither. Another aspect frequently overlooked is the organizational environment. Are signs and pamphlets readily available in different languages? Reception areas should make people from a variety of cultures feel welcome.

• documenting the existence of an ongoing social problem; connecting the immediate local concrete needs to a larger social issue gets back to our discussion on underlying causes. Homelessness may be the problem, but an underlying cause is poverty.

To this list, Dudley (2009: 112) adds determining the adequacy of existing informal resources. He points out that pressing needs are often addressed by informal resources, such as the extended family, neighbourhood associations, service clubs, churches, synagogues and mosques. Dudley adds that informal resources are often the first line of defence and the easiest for the client to approach. Whether the people needing help are young children, young single parents, older adults or people living with mental illness or developmental and physical disabilities, almost all of us rely on the help of family or other informal supports at different times during our lives. The question may be: What type of supports are needed by informal caregivers as they provide help?

While needs assessments are most often used to determine if a new program is required, a needs assessment can answer other questions as well (Dudley 2010: 321–23). Before determining if a new program or intervention is needed, it is be important to look at existing programs or interventions to find out if they are meeting the need and, if not, why not. This may involve a program evaluation of existing programs. Existing programs may meet the needs of some people but not others. For example, a study exploring whether pets were a barrier to women fleeing abusive relationships found that the rules of women's shelters varied as to whether they would allow women to bring their pets with them. Rules forbidding pets meet the needs of women with pet allergies or animal fears, but they do not meet the needs of women who take their pets for comfort or for fear that they will be abused. A needs assessment may (and in this situation did) find that there are not enough shelters that allow pets to accommodate women who want to keep their pets as well as themselves safe from harm. It is also possible that the existing programs are effective but lack needed follow-up programs. For example, a women's shelter may provide an excellent service but lack the resources to assist women leaving the shelter in finding second-stage housing.

Types of Needs Assessments

While most needs assessments involve some type of descriptive research, the choice of design depends on a few important questions. The following four key questions may help researchers choose their design (Marlow 2005):

1. Whose Need Is Being Assessed?

There are four levels of needs to be studied: the individual client, the organization, the community and the society. The same social problem may result in needs that are viewed very differently at each of the four levels. For instance, looking at our example of homelessness, the individual client may have a need to find safe, affordable housing. A community health centre may see its role as providing health care to people where they are living on the street. It may see its role as proving a shower, laundry and computer to give homeless people access to the internet to stay in contact with family members. The centre would need resources to be able to provide these services. The community may have a need to get homeless people off the streets in a cost effective way so as to involve the least amount of taxpayer dollars. Finally, society may have a need to ensure that all of its citizens are productive and not a drain on health and social services or feel a collective responsibility towards people who are suffering.

2. Who Will Have Input into the Design of the Needs Assessment?

This question is related to the previous one on whose need is being assessed. As structural social workers, we should be most concerned with meeting individual clients' needs (as well as changing societal structures that give rise to these needs). Therefore, a participatory approach should be used to achieve maximum client input and ownership. If clients are involved in research, the results will most likely be much more relevant and effective. An advisory committee can provide input into the design of the survey if a participatory approach is not possible.

3. When Will the Needs Assessment Be Carried Out?

In determining the timing of the research, there are two main designs: cross-sectional and longitudinal. The cross-sectional design is a survey that is carried out at one point in time. The Canadian census is an example of a cross-sectional design because Canadians all over the country complete the census form at the same time. The longitudinal design is research that is carried out on multiple occasions over an extended period of time. It describes processes occurring over a certain time period. The groups of people who live in proximity to and use the services of a community health centre can change over time. A centre wanting to assess whether it is meeting the needs of its constituents can conduct focus groups every five to ten years to see if the needs of the community are changing. There are two types of longitudinal designs: 1) trend studies, which look at different groups of people from the same population at different times; and 2) cohort studies, which follow a specific group that is linked in some way or that has experienced the same life events over time. There are many kinds of cohorts, for example, birth (all those born between 2000 and 2010), disease, education, employment, family formation, etc.

4. What Type of Understanding of the Need Is Required?

Most needs assessments use a descriptive, quantitative design, most often a survey. As Marlow points out, most funding bodies prefer to see data presented numerically. Such surveys usually involve either a mailed questionnaire or interviews (telephone or face-to-face). They could also rely on secondary information, such as census data. Surveys can provide extensive but superficial information on large groups of people (more on surveys in the next section).

If a more in-depth understanding of a social problem is required (and at some stage it usually is), a qualitative approach should be considered. For instance, researchers could invite interested participants to give individual interviews or attend a focus group. Another method of collecting qualitative data is via a community forum, which involves holding a meeting with members of the community concerned about a given need (Rubin and Babbie 2008). The choice of participants may vary, but researchers should seek out key partners. In our example of homelessness, the key informants would be homeless people themselves, along with shelter workers, the police, health care professionals and possibly residents of the affected area. In addition to improving the richness of the data and, thus, the depth of understanding, stories provided by key informants have the potential to convince funders of the severity of the need. In an interview or focus group, one is more likely to get a in-depth picture of how the social problem impacts individuals. A homeless individual could explain how the loss of a job and large debts at a time of recession led to losing their apartment. In a community forum, individuals may not feel comfortable giving details of their lived experience of being homeless. This format allows for people to discuss homelessness in a less personal manner, find out how it impacts the community, be stimulated by what others have to say and think about ideas they may not have considered. They may not have realized that homeless people would want free access to the internet and how difficult it might be to stay connected with family members.

The Survey

Rubin and Babbie (2008) state that survey research is perhaps the most widely used method of data collection in the social sciences. The survey normally involves a quantitative approach and makes use of a sample of respondents.

Most commonly known as participants, respondents are the people from whom information is collected. In order for the survey information to meet empirical standards, a few important design criteria should be considered. The first is sampling. If we are trying to describe the needs of a large client population, we must ensure that the sample, the small group of clients from which information will be collected, is representative of all those clients. In this way, findings are generalizable to the larger group. Usually, previous research can provide a great deal of information about the characteristics of the group under study. For example, research might give some idea of the number of homeless families versus the number of single people who are homeless. The researcher needs to ensure that the proportion of home-less families in the study is similar to the proportion in the population of the city being studied. This allows the findings to be generalizable. Collecting a representative sample is done using a technique called random sample. If we have access to the names and contact information of all clients, we can use a simple random sample. This resembles putting all the names in a hat and picking out names for the study. The systematic random sample involves having a list of clients and choosing, for example, every tenth client on the list. In either of these ways, each client has an equal chance of being chosen for the sample.

Survey information is most often collected using a questionnaire. For a

Table 9-1 Self Esteem

		Frequency	Percent	Valid Percent	Cumulative Percent
Index of Self-Esteem	5.00	1	11.1	11.1	11.1
	6.00	2	22.2	22.2	33.3
	7.00	3	33.3	33.3	66.7
	8.00	2	22.2	22.2	88.9
	9.00	1	11.1	11.1	100.0
	Total	9	100.0	100.0	

Table 9-2 Group Return Cross-Tabulation Count

	Returned to Abuse (1.00)	Did Not Return to Abuse (2.00)	Total
Attended program (1.00)	2	8	10
Did not attend program (2.00)	7	3	10
Total	9	11	20

study to meet the scientific rigour of traditional empirical research,[3] the data collection instrument (the questionnaire) must be tested for reliability and validity. Reliability means that the questionnaire gives accurate information consistently over time. Validity means that the information gathered is the information we intended to collect. Quantitative research, like this, typically presents the information in the form of statistical descriptions. These descriptions can be done in a variety of ways, ranging from simple frequencies (such as in Table 9-1, which gives the frequencies of a group of clients on their self-esteem) or comparisons (often called cross-tabulations). This is shown in Table 9-2, which compares the number of women who return to an abusive partner after attending a group program on assertiveness to the number of women who returned after not attending the group program. Table 9-2 shows that only two out ten women returned to an abusive partner after attending the group versus seven out ten women who did not attend the group. We discuss how to create survey questions and statistical presentation in Chapter Eleven, on quantitative research.

Focus Groups

A focus group is a group of people who are interviewed together. This format allows discussion of the interview questions and can bring out aspects of a topic that researchers may not have anticipated and that may not emerge in individual interviews (Rubin and Babbie 2008). Focus groups are inexpensive, usually generate speedy results and offer flexibility for probing. One of our students noted that when discussing various methods of collecting data, advisory committee members preferred a focus group because "the communities have had too many surveys in their mailboxes so would likely not be willing to fill out another survey for this research."[4]

The disadvantages include that shyer participants might feel pressure to agree with more vocal members of the group rather than express dissenting opinions. For example, if community members are asked if they would use certain services, some people might go along with the crowd and say they would when in reality they would not use the service. Many authors suggest inviting six to ten participants to control for the potential problem of some not showing up for the actual focus group meeting (Bryman and Teevan 2005). Smaller groups are more appropriate when the topic is controversial or emotionally charged, and larger groups are more often utilized when the researcher wants to hear numerous brief suggestions (ibid). A focus group is facilitated by one of the researchers, often called the moderator. Fox, Martin and Green (2007) encourage the involvement of service users as co-moderators for focus groups. Involving service users in this way allows them to steer the research and be an active participant in the data collection. "The service user thus becomes a research participant, an active researcher and a research consultant. This approach may facilitate a shift from passive service user involvement to a more genuine collaboration" (144). Usually the moderator raises unstructured questions or topic areas with the group. Various options can be used to facilitate the order of participation, for example, a speakers list, participants raise their hands or participants take turns in a circle using a talking stick or other object.

A project in Manitoba explored the experiences of lesbians who have suffered abuse and queried what kinds of social services and support systems they would like to see developed. The following describes their focus group process:

> Participants met in small discussion groups with facilitators who taped-recorded and summarized on flip charts the responses to our questions. In addition to giving us important information, this method allowed for consciousness-raising about the issue of lesbian abuse and provided an opportunity for lesbians in various areas to learn about our project and perhaps organize a response themselves to the barriers and issues identified in their communities. (Ristock and Pennell 1996: 60)

Some researchers use a drama-based method as a variation of a focus group. Data is collected beforehand, and out of this initial data a performance emerges which involves a drama-based process of analysis and dissemination. There is no moderator and no division between the researcher and the participants within the context of a dramatic collective creation. Patricia Leavy provides the following example:

> Finley (1998) presented a Reader's Theatre piece based on interviews with homeless people in New Orleans. Out of these interviews Finley created composite character types of youth identified in the data. The dramatic presentation of the data, in which each character spoke in the first person, allowed Finley to get at some of the authentic experience in a way that would not have been possible with traditional representational forms. (2009: 142)

Focus group facilitators should follow a script that contains the following elements (Brun 2005: 140):

1. introductions of focus group leaders and a statement of the purpose of the focus group;
2. statement of conditions of the informed consent with each participant asked to sign the written form. Anonymity cannot be guaranteed in a focus group but participants can be asked to

not repeat what they hear in the focus group to anyone outside of it;

3. an explanation of the format of the focus group, for example, "I will give each of you a chance to answer a question if you choose to before I go on to the next one";
4. the actual interview guide questions, including probes; and
5. time for questions from the participants and to thank them and let them know how they can request results of the study.

The following tips will help with running a focus group:

- Make a checklist of all of the items that are needed for the focus group and check it before jumping in the car to travel to the venue.
- What is not said may be as important as what is said.
- Stick to the whatever timeframe is given to participants. People have busy schedules; they may be paying a babysitter or have to get to work.
- Include a wide range of participants, though they may need to be organized into separate groups, such as age, gender, education, having or not having had a certain experience (Bryman and Teevan 2005).
- If recording what participants say on a flip chart, do not change their words. If summarizing their words, check with them to make sure you captured what they meant to say.
- Use name tags as it allows you to call people by their name, which helps them feel recognized and more comfortable.
- Do not let one interviewee dominate the discussion, because this will inhibit others from sharing their opinions.
- Resist over-directing the focus group and thereby bringing your own views into play.

Environmental Scans

Another important method for conducting needs assessments is the environmental scan. This technique considers the factors that will influence client needs. It involves gathering, analyzing and dispensing information for tactical or strategic purposes. In the United States a school district designed an environmental scan to obtain a multi-dimensional reading of the need for mental health services, as a preliminary step toward the implementation of a mental health case management program in all local schools (Cohen and Angeles 2006). An environmental scan includes looking at the present factors, such as the current extent of the needs, but also future trends, since needs may change over time. Another research project, looking at how to improve services for new moms with mental health problems, engaged in an environmental scan that included discussions with service users, community mental health clinicians, consumers, general practitioners and midwives. As a result a framework was developed to determine how to best help mothers with mental health problems when they are home with their newborn babies (Hauck, Rock, Jackiewicz and Jablensky 2008). A project in British Columbia utilized an environmental scan to assess the capacity of organizations working with individuals diagnosed with HIV/AIDS to engage in community-based research (Ibanez-Carrasco 2004). The scan included interviews, site visits, case studies, participant observation and "social marketing." This later component included placing articles in magazines and doing public presentations to promote and educate people about the services of the capacity-building community-based research program (Ibanez-Carrasco 2004).

There has been a dramatic increase in the number of homeless families with children over the last few years. In our example about homelessness, an environmental scan could consider, among other things, government policy changes that affect the type and extent of programs and services serving the homeless. While the federal and provincial governments have done very little to combat homelessness in the last few decades, if a policy change outlines a renewed commitment to invest in low-cost housing, the extent of homelessness among families may quickly change.

A Carleton University student research group conducted a needs assessment that included a variation on an environmental scan. An organization which was offering a day program serving young single parents was interested in knowing if their facility was located in an area of town that made it readily accessible to the majority of their clients. Using the postal codes of the clients' home addresses, the student researchers were able to plot clients' locations on a map. They also looked at bus routes to determine how clients with kids and strollers were able to get to the program. They plotted the location of other services that the clients would likely need. In this way, they were able to make recommendations for the best and most accessible location for the program facility.

The Strength-Based Approach

In this chapter, we have been using the term "needs assessment" because it is common in social work research. As structural social workers, though, we recognize that the term "needs" orients us towards the negative characteristics of clients; we look at what clients are missing while ignoring what they have. Focusing on the negative rather than the positive may be doing clients a disservice, as we may inadvertently underestimate the capacity of our clients to choose what is best for themselves.

It is out of this reasoning that the strength-based approach developed. While there are no specific strength-based techniques, Tuula Heinonen and Leonard Spearman (2001) describe this approach as facilitating "people's own resources to help them meet four goals: 1) to grow as human beings, 2) to improve their quality of life, 3) to develop their own problem-solving skills, and 4) to deal with their stress and adversity" (213). The authors contrast this with the traditional focus of mainstream social work on pathologizing and correcting existing problems. They see the strength-based approach as a "frontal attack on efforts to treat personal and social problems as pathologies or deficits" (212). Marion Bogo (2006) sees the strength-based approach as a way to mitigate against the power imbalances between those seeking help and those providing it by reinforcing client competence and aiding in collaboration. In this conception, social workers are much more "helpers" and facilitators, than experts who can correct inadequate behaviour in people who have troubles.

The strength-based approach is not really new. A problem-solving approach has always included acknowledging client strengths. For example, Beulah Compton and Burt Gallaway (1999: 7) write that "developing a solution to the problem will call upon the strengths brought by the client, you, and the environment. Thus the problem-solving model is strength focused." But rather than focusing on problem solving, the strength-based approach may highlight peoples' strengths more dramatically.

This approach fits well with the structural perspective, which attempts to maximize client self-determination. While the worker continues in an advisory capacity, the client is in control of the process. Clients are viewed as individuals capable of making decisions that are in their best interests. Clients can choose whether or not they need help and who provides it.

Heinonen and Spearman (2001) acknowledge that allowing the client to be in control is more difficult with involuntary clients, such as people involved with child protection or the criminal justice system. However, while the law places restrictions on the flexibility workers have in giving control to certain clients, there are always areas where even involuntary clients can have decision-making power.

The goal of the strength-based approach is for clients to make decisions affecting their lives. By focusing on strengths as opposed to "needs," we identify solutions that are much more in keeping with the structural perspective than in the traditional social work approach.

Community Capacity in a Low-Income Housing Project

A team of Carleton University MSW students sought to develop a "capacity inventory" to identify the strengths of people living in a low-income housing project (Canteenwalla, Eagle, Phelps and Zapotochny 2006). The specific objectives of the research were to identify such things as job skills, education levels, current employment, talents and language skills. This information helps to identify the assets that individual members of the community possess which could potentially be resources for the rest of the community. The students were also interested in knowing if residents were willing to volunteer and lend their skills to the community.

In choosing their theoretical framework, the students looked at the following two different approaches to mapping community capacity: 1) identifying existing community capacity and 2) assessing needs. The students agreed that the traditional "needs-oriented solution" is based on the belief that the community is deficient. In contrast, identifying community capacity is a process that stems from within the community as community members themselves identify individual and community assets. The goal of this approach is to create an inventory of assets in order to begin a process that maximizes the potential of the community.

In order to maximize community control, the students worked with community partners. The community had a community house that provided programs such as child care, language and skill upgrading classes and social activities. The community also had an active tenants' association run by a board of directors made up of community residents. The purpose of the tenants' association was to establish policies and rules for the community house.

All aspects of the research methodology, including the data collection instrument, were presented to the tenants' association for approval. The data collection involved conducting a survey of the entire community and a quantitative descriptive design supplemented by some open-ended qualitative questions. Roughly two thirds of the residents completed the survey. See Appendix 4 for the survey instrument, which was developed and approved by the tenants' association (the name of the association has been changed for confidentiality).

DISCUSSION QUESTIONS

1. Why is it important to look at underlying needs?
2. What are the pros and cons of involving client or community members in conducting needs assessments?
3. Whose needs normally take priority; the clients, the staff and administration, the community or the funders? Explain.
4. What are the advantages and disadvantages of an advisory committee?
5. From a strength-based perspective, why is the term "needs assessment" problematic?

Notes

1. Sarah Pederson, "The Push and Pull of Research Methods: A Reflexive Journal," unpublished, Carleton University, November 2010.
2. With respect to networking skills, social workers have access to a range of networking tools, such as our Blue Book in Ottawa, which is a directory of all health and social services, on-line directories, websites for municipal services,

which normally include useful internet links, as well as access to knowledgeable people such as colleagues and other professionals.

3. The concern with scientific rigour is to ensure that if this is the method the research team has chosen to meet a certain political goal, it must be conducted in a way to be believable and convincing.

4. Christine Howey, Reflexive Journal 2, January 2011.

10. Qualitative Methods

Once the research question has been selected and approved by the research partners, the next set of decisions involves the method or methods of data collection and analysis. This is a crucial step because the usefulness of the conclusions will depend on the methods chosen. Client and organizational members of the advisory committee can play an invaluable role in developing the methods of collecting and analyzing data that best lead to the desired social change (Brun 2005; Kirby et al. 2006).

Social work researchers following a structural perspective use both quantitative and qualitative methods. Quantitative methods are normally associated with the more traditional positivist and empiricist approach while qualitative methods are associated with the more progressive post-positivist and interpretivist approach (Marlow 2005). What distinguishes the structural social work researcher from others is not the research method chosen but the amount of decision-making power clients and other research partners have on the methods chosen. For example, a research group that wants to convince a funder to build affordable housing needs to decide which method will best help reach that goal. Some funders are most convinced by statistics that document the number of people who are homeless, health care costs due to illness caused by a lack of affordable housing, etc. Other funders may be more convinced by hearing about the toll it takes on homeless people and their families because they cannot access affordable housing. Many funders might be best convinced by both. Either way, the research team should base its decision about the best research methodology based on which is more likely to help attain the social change goal. The question that researchers need to ask is: will the research help to promote the social changes that clients are requesting?

Differences between Quantitative and Qualitative Methods

As stated above, quantitative methods are normally associated with the positivist approach. The categories of the research topic under investigation, that is, the items to be measured, are chosen prior to the study (Marlow 2005; Faulkner and Faulkner 2009). Numerical values are assigned to these categories and the data is analyzed statistically. The following question, taken from a survey on the service needs of lesbian, gay, bisexual, trans, two-spirited, queer (LGBTTQ) families, demonstrates how items may be given a numerical value and analyzed.

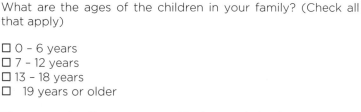

What are the ages of the children in your family? (Check all that apply)

☐ 0 – 6 years
☐ 7 – 12 years
☐ 13 – 18 years
☐   19 years or older

The LGBTTQ families represented in the survey had an average of two children each. In fact, the large majority of families had only one or two children (32.3% and 35.5% respectively). A smaller number (12.9%) of families had three children. In addition, one family had four children, one family had five children and one family had six children. The ages of the children in the families participating ranged widely. However, more families had children in the younger age brackets: from 0 to 6 years (51.6%) and from 7 to 12 years (35.5%). In the older age groups, 29% of families had children who were aged 13 to 18 years, and 25.8% of families had children who were 19 years or older.[1]

Qualitative methods are generally associated with the interpretivist approach and involve a non-numerical examination of the research topic. Qualitative methods often rely on a small number of participants and the analysis tends to take a narrative approach. Leslie Tutty, Michael Rothery and Richard Grinnell (1996: 13) provide an excellent example of the strength of qualitative research:

> Qualitative researches will often prefer to represent information in non-numerical forms, such as texts (words) or images. These kinds of representation are better suited to capturing and communicating the complexities and subtleties of human experiences. Instead on analyzing such data statistically, qualitative researchers may study a text for meaningful elements, look for similarities and differences between them, and establish how elements can fit into categories and establish how these categories can form more general themes.

While quantitative methods continue to have a strong following, social work knowledge is derived largely from qualitative data analysis. Basic qualitative methods include unstructured interviews, analyses of client files and case studies. In general, quantitative methods gather information that is wide and shallow, and qualitative methods gather information that is narrow and deep. Both kinds of information are necessary for structural social work, knowledge creation and good science. One of our students put into her own words the benefits of qualitative research:

> As a researcher I feel that I am putting myself in the position of a consumer of peoples' thoughts, emotions, joys and pains and while intimidated by what a big responsibility that is, I am also humbled by the generosity of individuals who agree to partici-pate in research. The fact that people will be giving some part of themselves to me, a stranger, who may or may not "get it right" and may or may not listen effectively, reminds me how important it is to chose a methodology that honours the con-tribution of participants and contributes in some small way to the body of knowledge that informs interventions in their lives and the lives of others.[2]

Qualitative Research Interview

The most common data collection method in qualitative research is the interview, which is simply a form of directed conversation (Rubin and Babbie 2008). The purpose of the interview is to gain an understanding of the perspective of the person being interviewed, to learn about a person's experiences, thoughts and feelings from their point of view (Tutty, Rothery and Grinnell 1996).

There are three types of interviews; structured, unstructured and semi-structured. Structured interviews, also called "standardized interviews," involve requesting information through specific questions that are identical for every person being interviewed (Rubin and Babbie 2008). The interviewer is encouraged not to deviate from a script or to change the order of the questions. In unstructured interviews, sometimes called "informal conversational interviews," all the possible questions are not known in advance but emerge as the interview progresses. Semi-structured interviews are between the above two extremes and involve the use of an interview guide, where the order of questions may vary depending on the flow of the interview (Neuman and Robson 2009). The main advantage of structured and semi-structured inter-views is they allow for comparisons between interviews; the main disadvantage is that the exploration of unanticipated themes is limited. For example, a researcher assessing the benefits of a mental health service user-run business (e.g., a bike courier business) may ask questions that measure developing good work habits, an increased sense of self worth, added ability to purchase things, feeling more connected to society and making friends. The results of a structured interview might allow us to make statements about how many participants felt that their sense of self worth was increased. However, we may not have anticipated that some of the participants saw losing weight as one of the benefits of being a bike courier. Open-ended questions allow for better collection of unanticipated answers.

Another type of interview used frequently in qualitative data collection is the focus group. James Dudley describes the focus group as "a special type of group interview that takes on the characteristics of structured and unstructured interviews" (2010: 231–32). He identifies a number of principles and procedures in conducting focus groups. Some of these include:

- General questions are introduced to provide a focus or purpose.
- All the participants share their views in response to the questions.
- Everyone has an adequate amount of time to share.
- No one debates each other.
- Differences are respected.
- The facilitator keeps the group focused on the topic and makes sure that everyone has a chance to share their views.
- The recorder writes down everyone's comments.
- After everyone has shared, the recorder reads everyone's comments to make sure they are accurate and to encourage additional clarification.
- The group looks for common themes among the views that have been shared.
- The results are organized into a report.

In the research course we teach, we encourage two students to act as moderators when running a focus group, one to lead the discussion and the other to record important parts of the discussion. A team of students was running a group activity with high school youth who were instructed to create collages to illustrate barriers to success in school. The youth were each asked to present their collage, which initiated discussion with other youth. A fuller discussion of focus groups is in the preceding chapter, on needs assessments.

Issues in Qualitative Interviewing

Tutty, Rothery and Grinnell (1996) identified the following three issues that must be considered before interviewing: 1) the equality of the research relationship; 2) dealing with strong emotions during the interview; and 3) the distinction between qualitative research interviewing and therapeutic interviewing. With respect to the first, the nature of the relationship between interviewer and interviewee has changed in recent years. In the past, interviewers were required to keep their distance in order to remain neutral and objective and to remain in control of the interview (Gregg 1994). Today, the relationship is more equal and interactive, with interviewers regarding interviewees as experts in terms of their unique perspectives. At the same time, interviewers are trained to be cognizant of their own perspectives on issues of race, gender and class and how these might affect their relationship with an interviewee. This is more difficult than it appears at first glance. As we alluded to in an earlier chapter, to help interviewers get in touch with their perspectives, they need to engage in reflexive exercises (Tutty, Rothery and Grinnell 1996). This more equal interview relationship is consistent with semi- and unstructured interviews. There is less room for fostering interactive relationships in structured interviews.

The next issue involves dealing with strong emotions. There is the potential for strong emotions to result when interviewees are sharing critical events in their lives. Interviewers need to be supportive and allow interviewees time to regain their composure. You can offer the participant a drink of water, a short break and empathy. If the interviewee is unable to regain their composure, the interviewer must be prepared to stop the interview (Tutty, Rothery and Grinnell 1996). Role-playing the interview with other members of the research team or advisory group can prepare an interviewer for handling strong emotions. Training from more experienced interviewers can also be helpful.

In terms of the last issue that may affect the interview, the interview must be clear about the similarities and differences between research interviews and therapeutic interviews. They are similar in that the interviewee is encouraged to express private thoughts and observations, recalling and reflecting on memories. But there are also three important differences. First, the goal of qualitative interviewing is to collect useful data and not to promote individual change. Second, interviewees are asked to share personal stories only to the extent that it meets the purpose of the study. Third, interviewers and interviewees form an information gathering partnership rather than a helping partnership (Tutty, Rothery and Grinnell 1996).

A student in our class consulted with us about whether she needed to take action following one of her interviews. Her group was interviewing social workers about the best practices in working with traumatized women. Our student was concerned that these social workers were experiencing vicarious traumatization without knowing it and required counselling. She wondered who she should inform about this. The implicit contract between this student and the research participant involved gathering information. The researcher saw "vicarious traumatization of the workers" as a theme that arose in her data analysis, but it was not her responsibility to provide counselling for these workers. This does not mean that the researcher does not show empathy for the research participant.

Below, two students share in their reflexive journals how they understand the difference between a therapeutic interview and a research interview. The first quote is from a student who conducted research on intimate partner violence. The second student ran focus groups to gain information for a needs assessment for a local community health centre.

I found it difficult when interviewees would express a particular view that I would challenge in a therapeutic interview or as
part of an educational activism piece. For example, one of the
interviewees expressed that sexual orientation was irrelevant
to the experience of the victims. As a social worker I wanted
to educate the agency about intersecting oppressions, the way
sexual orientation impacts all aspects of an individual's life and
the struggles the community faces as a result. However, our
purpose was to collect data, not promote change.[3]

While the ultimate goal of community-based research is to promote
change, it is often challenging to understand when the change component
takes places. What do you do in an interview when your values and theoretical perspective differ from the person you are interviewing? The interviewee
has agreed to give you information; they have not necessarily agreed to
consciousness-raising. If, as an interviewer, you strongly vocalize a difference
of opinion, the participant may feel embarrassed and humiliated and withdraw their interview from the project. It is better to use all of the data that
is collected and provide the education for social change in the final report.

I became increasingly aware of my tendency to interact with (the
focus group) participants in a "therapeutic" manner. I found it
extremely difficult to occupy the role of neutral researcher, and
had to work hard to restrain myself from engaging participants
on an emotional level. For example, I frequently found myself
paraphrasing participants' responses, identifying common emotional themes, and offering my interpretation of what was being
said. As a social worker, this is what I have been trained to do, and
I found it difficult to contain my desire to connect with the participants on a deeper level. Similarly, I found it difficult to restrain
my personal responses when participants said something that
resonated with me internally. I caught myself leaning forward,
smiling, and asking them to elaborate in an encouraging tone.
I even went so far as to offer my thoughts on the matter. As a
therapeutic group facilitator, this might be acceptable, but as a
researcher, this type of encouragement may influence the type
of information that participants are willing to share.[4]

While leaning forward, smiling and encouraging participants to speak
are not bad things to do in a focus group, both students were struggling with
the amounts of encouragement and consciousness-raising that are productive for the interview or focus group and how much might taint the research
results. It is important to ask the questions and reflect upon what you as a
researcher feel comfortable with. There is no right or wrong answer.

Preparing for the Interview

In terms of preparing for the interview, the first task is personal preparation. As Tutty, Rothery and Grinnell (1996) point out, qualitative interviewing is stressful and demanding. This process is similar to what Lawrence Shulman (1999) calls "tuning in" when preparing for a social work interview. Prepare yourself for what might be difficult parts of the interview so you are best able to ask the required questions. For example, in research exploring the lived experiences of sex trade workers, the interviewer would need to feel comfortable talking about non-traditional sexual practices. If you do not feel that this is a legitimate form of employment, then you would need to consider how your opinions might affect the interview and how you can mediate against these effects.

Second, you should plan to keep a personal journal to record your thoughts, feelings and reactions throughout the process. This journal will help to identify how your perspective (and biases) influenced the interview. This becomes very useful during the data analysis phase. Third, you need to rid yourself of your own biases as much as possible, a process known as "epoch." Using the above example, identifying squeamishness about talking about sexual practices and how you would overcome this squeamishness is working towards epoch. Interviewers must achieve as much epoch as possible. As a general strategy, it is a good idea to role-play or pre-test the interview (Tutty, Rothery and Grinnell 1996).

The next task is to think about the type and number of participants needed for the study. There are two distinct categories of interviewees. If you want to study the experiences of people who share something in common, you need to interview a sample of people who represent the phenomenon in question. In the above example, exploring the lived experience of women who work in the sex trade, these would be the women you would need to interview. If, on the other hand, you want to learn about a topic or event, you need to interview experts in the area or witnesses to the event. Interviewers need to be persistent but, at the same time, use sensitivity and tact to gain access to interviewees. Finding interviewees may involve finding someone, possibly who acts as a gate-keeper, who can refer you to others (Tutty, Rothery and Grinnell 1996).

In terms of the number of participants needed for the study, in qualitative research it is difficult to give a definitive number prior to conducting interviews. The general rule is that you keep interviewing until no new information is forthcoming. This is the point when you have reached theme redundancy and no new themes are likely to emerge (Brun 2005). It is up to you as the researcher, often in consultation with an advisory committee or research partners in PAR research, to determine when you have reached this point.

The third task is preparing the interviewee. Once you have received ethics clearance, you should contact the potential interviewee and explain in detail who you are, the purpose and nature of the research, what is expected of the interviewee, the potential risks and benefits, the limits of confidentiality and whether follow-up interviews are required. All of this information should be included in a consent letter to be signed by the interviewee.

Finally, prior to beginning the interview, you should also decide on the recording method. The most common method is to audio record the interview using a tape recorder. The nature of qualitative research requires that you record what the participant is saying as fully as possible (Rubin and Babbie 2008). A method used by many researchers is taking notes during the interview, sometimes in addition to tape recording (Patton 1990, cited in Rubin and Babbie 2008), as note-taking safeguards against mechanical failure. If the interviewee is uncomfortable about note-taking, offer to show what you have written. If two researchers interview, one person could conduct the interview while the other records the responses (Tutty, Rothery and Grinnell 1996). Some researchers write up a detailed set of notes after the interview. This method, often used in social work supervision, is called process recording (Sheafor, Horejsi and Horejsi 1991). It should be done immediately after the interview while the information is still fresh in the mind of the researcher. Often two (or more) columns are used, one to record, almost verbatim, what was said and the other for reflexive comments. Reflexive comments written after the interview allow the researcher to record impressions, reactions, hunches and general comments.[5]

The Interview

Effective interviewing depends to a great extent on being able to establish a positive dynamic. It is helpful to begin an interview with a few minutes of small talk. Berg (2004) suggests that if you are in the person's home, look around, comment on photographs. Make sure that the interviewee is comfortable and that you can conduct the interview without being overheard. Always be respectful and assure the interviewee that their opinions are important to you and the project. At the beginning of an interview, keep the demographic questions to a minimum (you can always ask more demographic questions at the end of the interview) and use open-ended questions in a language familiar to the interviewee. It is important to ensure that each question focuses on one thought. If you are interviewing people from other cultures, be aware of cultural differences between yourself and the interviewee. Allan Rubin and Earl Babbie call this "culturally competent research," which they define as "research that is sensitive and responsive to the ways in which cultural factors and cultural differences influence what we investigate, how we investigate, and how we interpret our findings" (2010: 274). For example, a group of students conducted a needs assessment for a local community health centre that was concerned about providing services to new immigrants from the Caribbean and Africa. In recruiting participants, the researchers put up posters in areas frequented by these immigrants. They reviewed their questions with their advisory committee, which included members of that community. Lastly, they made sure that they would have a translator present for participants whose primary language is French.

Some authors identify providing adequate compensation to participants as another aspect of culturally competent research. Rubin and Babbie (2010) believe that while providing compensation is important for all participants, it is crucial when they are members of groups that experience poverty and marginalization. Norton and Manson (1996) add that compensation may not be limited to individual participants; for example, compensation for the entire community should be considered in Aboriginal communities. Compensation might be monetary, large enough to provide an incentive but not so large as to be considered coercive. A group of students investigating the benefits of mental health service user businesses thought that $15 would not be enough incentive. After discussing this with their advisory committee, they realized that this amount would be significant for their target participant group. Compensation can also be in the form of food, gift cards or a coffee. The group that conducted the focus group for the community health centre arranged for a local African catering group to prepare culturally appropriate finger food for the focus group participants.

At the appropriate time, signal that the interview is coming to an end. You can bring closure by summarizing what was covered. At this point you should ask for additional information not covered by your questions. A good practice is to offer to show transcribed notes. You then need to thank the interviewee and, if necessary, make arrangement for follow-up interviews. If the interview was particularly difficult on the interviewee, you should make arrangements for a meeting with a mental health counsellor.

It is important to reflect on the interview. Reflection will inform your decisions at each step of the way. You can record your reflections during the interview. Social workers often take notes while they are interviewing the people they work with. You can show your notes to the research participant so they can ensure the veracity of what you are recording. Some researchers find it more helpful to find a quiet place after the interview and record their impressions, reflections and anything that the participants said that they do not feel they captured during the interview. Tutty, Rothery and Grinnell suggest asking the following questions. "Is this information really needed for [the] study? Is the information of a high enough quality that I can use it in [the] study?" (1996: 80). Carefully record these decisions in your journal. Review the impact of your decisions and actions once the interview is over. Without reflection, your study may be unfocused.

Qualitative Data Analysis

Once all the interviewing is over, the next major phase of the research process involves data analysis. Keep in mind that the goal of qualitative data analysis is to develop an in-depth understanding of the personal realities of the participants. You should try to understand their reality in as much complexity as possible.

The first major step in the analysis involves transcribing the interview. This is an onerous task as each interview can result in thirty to fifty pages of transcribed text. The next major step is choosing the method of analysis. The most common method involves the traditional cut-and-paste method, where you literally cut typed sections of the transcribed interview, such as groups of words, sentences or paragraphs, and organize these manually into categories. An increasingly popular method is to use a computer program such as N Vivo, developed by QSR International. Programs like this can assist in sorting and organizing data.

You are now ready to begin the analysis. As a first step, you must read over all the transcribed material so that you get a sense of the data as a whole. Continue to use the research journal that you started during the interview phase to record all decisions, ideas and insights, and the context of each idea and insight that you have during this phase of the research. This provides an "audit trail," to be used in the event that your analysis is questioned, and contributes to the overall trustworthiness of your results (Tutty, Rothery and Grinnell 1996). It is also useful to identify any biases that might be creeping in and ensure that you have truly understood what the participants have said.

Figure 10-1 Analyzing Qualitative Data: Process Involving Constant Comparisons

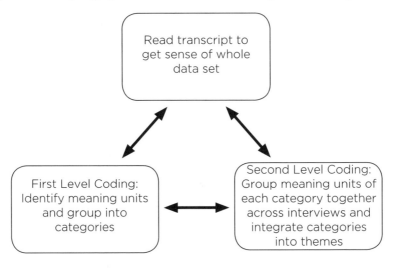

First Level Coding

Tutty, Rothery and Grinnell (1996) see the analysis as being divided into two levels of coding. The first level involves identifying meaning units (some call these "message units" [Padgett 2004]), which can be words, a sentence or part of a paragraph and form the building blocks of the analysis. Next, decide how the meaning units relate to one another. Group the related meaning units into categories and assign a name and code (one or two letters) to each category. Below is a compilation of a number of transcripts from field supervisors talking about their experience of working with social work students. In the first answer to the researcher's question, the concept of allowing students to practise structural social work is an important meaning unit. The category that it might fit into is "students getting to practise in a manner consistent with their education." In the second answer the category unit might be "the multiple challenges that the people we work with experience."

> What do you think your placement offers students that might not be available in other placements?
>
> I think the approach of working with adult women is really quite unique especially in the addictions field. So I think what the student gets is a very unique opportunity to see structural social work at its... well.... I wouldn't say at its best because we are human, we make mistakes too. But it is a very healthy delivery.... that's what happens, it is a very healthy delivery of the concept of structural social work in terms of just how to work with adult women, like how to respect them as equals. We have different responsibilities but to be working with them as human beings with all the resources that they need and they just need some support to get to where they want. So as much as we can we try to... we hope that the student would get to see.... wow this is how you work with people and that you hear where they are and you hear where they want to go and you just help them navigate and identify what they need to do to get to where they want to be. So I think very non-judgmental environment here. We really appreciate that every staff member is very different and the thing that students bring that is really for the residents to see is that — wow if this women can be working so hard on her education and you know managing all of her life things as well then maybe I can do that too. That sort of, kind of a nice little advantage that we receive from having students here. But I think the best of what the students gets here is just the seeing the heart of social work being played out day after day in a very respectful environment.
>
> And would you also like to comment on the kind of clientele that they are exposed compared to other placement agencies?
>
> Sure. The women who come here have challenges with sobriety.

Many of them are on Ontario Works so they have very meagre incomes. Many women have worked in the sex trade, have lived on the streets. I would say the majority of the women have been involved in some degree or another with the sex trade — either the dancing or the actual prostitution. Several women are involved with criminal activity. And that's another intriguing treatment aspect — criminal activity as a result of using or criminal activity when using at the same time, so it is a little bit different. So sort of like the women who are really marginalized — the Inuit women, the Native women — who we would very commonly see on the streets will often end up here. Women who come here from the homeless shelters.[6]

Organizing meaning units into categories can be done using a method called "constant comparisons" (Tutty, Rothery and Grinnell 1996: 103). It begins once the entire data set has been examined and the meaning units have been identified. Each unit is classified as either similar or different from others. Record your observations about why units are similar in your journal. Repeat these steps until all meaning units have been classified. Some meaning units may not be easily classified into a category. You may need to collect these in a category called miscellaneous, but record why these units do not fit in your other categories. If too many units end up in the miscellaneous bin, you will need to re-examine your categories. Some meaning units could fit in different categories while others overlap. You must constantly re-examine your choice of categories to ensure you are examining your data in its complexity. If after interviewing new participants, the meaning units fit easily into existing categories and no new categories emerge, it is time to stop. You have reached the redundancy or "category saturation" stage (Tutty, Rothery and Grinnell 1996: 106).

In terms of identifying categories, Rubin and Babbie (2008) suggest there are two possible types of perspectives. Emic perspectives are the points of view of the people being studied and result in the indigenous-created categories. In other words, emic perspectives include the language/terms used by the participants. The second type is the etic perspective, which includes the research-constructed categories or those the researcher applies to the data. The emic and etic perspectives will differ owing to differences between the participant and the researcher in value systems, gender, age, race and ethnicity. For example, we conducted a study of social work field supervisors to determine how they measured quality in a field placement. The field supervisors evaluated quality in terms of how well the student fit with the supervisor and the team and into the smooth running of the agency. They might call this category "goodness of fit." As a researcher, I found that when the student and the field supervisor "operated from the same theoretical perspective," usually a structural social work perspective, the placement was of a higher quality. In evaluating the data we could use categories that arose from the participants (emic categories) or the ones we deduced (etic perspective). Most people who engage in qualitative research view the emic-etic distinction and the possibility of multiple interpretations of the same event as an opportunity rather than a constraint (Yin, 2011). This highlights the importance of involving service users in all aspects of the research. Their different perspective increases the opportunity of fuller results.

Second Level Coding

The second level of coding is more abstract and involves data interpretation. The first step in this level involves retrieving the meaning units of each category and grouping them together across interviews. All the meaning units which fit within category one should be grouped together. The same goes for category two and so on. This separates the meaning units from the interview.

The next step is to compare and contrast the categories themselves in order to discover the relationships between them. The goal here is to integrate the categories into themes and sub-themes based on their properties. Finding themes involves locating patterns that appear in your data. Once a theme is identified, develop a code for it in the same manner as you coded categories. The themes will form the basis of the major conclusions from your analysis. You are now ready to write up your results.

Trustworthiness

Rubin and Babbie (2010) acknowledge that trustworthiness means different things depending on the paradigm the researcher operates from. For those concerned with evidence-based practice, trustworthiness refers to the rigour of a qualitative study, the extent to which steps were taken to lessen the effects of the researcher's bias and subjectivity. From a PAR perspective, establishing trustworthiness includes showing whether participants were empowered by the research. There are four elements of trustworthiness: credibility, transferability, dependability and confirmability (Bryman and Teevan 2005).

Credibility refers to how believable the findings are, or the extent to which the researchers were careful to not let their biases influence the results. Transferability refers to whether the findings can apply to other similar contexts. Dependability asks if the findings will be consistent over time. Lastly, confirmability occurs when another member of the research team, including service users if PAR techniques are employed, reaches the same conclusions about the findings. When not employing PAR techniques, you can still get feedback from participants about your findings, which is referred to as member checking (Brun 2005; Tutty, Rothery and Grinnell 1996). Because qualitative research depends on personal judgment, you must indicate why you should be believed. Consistency is a key to establishing believability. You must be rigorous in interviewing and in developing the rules for coding. Another researcher should be able to follow your process and come to the same conclusions. Some interviews provide more information than others, so you should specify and record your interview weighting scheme.

Triangulation refers to seeking corroboration between two or more sources and using multiple methods to obtain a more thorough view of the subject. One use of triangulation is to ask a colleague, possibly one who holds a different theoretical orientation or who is from a different discipline, to use your data collection rules and verify your conclusions (Berg 2007). Janice Ristock and Joan Pennell (1996) give this description of triangulation done as part of a PhD thesis exploring feminist social service collectives:

> My research journey was a reflexive process of triangulating methods in response to findings as I proceeded. The national survey provided necessary descriptive information — a snapshot of what was happening across Canada; the document analysis provided insights into the public profile of collectives and the strong link between feminist values and the collective structure; and the interviews elicited personal accounts that provided in-depth and critical information about the contradictory and complex culture of collectives. (56)

While journaling, you can make an inventory of your biases and continually check to see if these influenced your conclusions.

Akosua Agyei-Amoama et al. (2008: 16, 17) describe how they ensure consistency and trustworthiness:

- Research team members are all passionate about the subject. We therefore exercised dedication and professional commitment to the research.
- There was consistency in communication amongst the research team members.
- Reflexivity: the two reflexive papers helped keep us in constant reflection on all aspects of the research process and on things that were not working.
- We held regular research meetings to discuss and to make team decisions.
- We made sure that the focus group time was sufficient and used well to ensure we got enough rich data.
- The data analysis process was very rigorous – we spent a lot of time discussing, and disagreeing before reaching any agreement.

DISCUSSION QUESTIONS

1. Do you believe that qualitative research is a valid means of knowledge development?
2. Are qualitative methods only useful in certain situations or with certain kinds of research questions?
3. What do you think would be the most difficult thing for you if you were to conduct a qualitative interview?

Notes

1. Example drawn from Shannon Sommerauer, Kate Hanton, Shellie Bird, "Around the Rainbow Project Report," March 31, 2010.
2. Jaime Lenet, Reflexive Journal 1, November 2010.
3. Catherine Brohman, Reflexive Journal, 2011.
4. David Adam, Reflexive Journal II, January 25, 2011.
5. A more complete list of suggestions is provided by Tutty, Rothery and Grinnell (1996: 70).
6. Karen Schwartz, Research project, Faculty of Social Work, Carleton University, 2005.

11. Quantitative Methods

While quantitative methods clearly fit within the positivist paradigm, structural social work researchers will in all likelihood need to use statistics in developing sound arguments to advocate for meaningful social change. As expressed by Victor Thiessen in his book *Arguing with numbers* (1993: 3), "the ever-increasing invasion of statistics is now part of our lives, regardless of how we feel about it." Without question, research from a structural perspective can and does use "traditional" quantitative methods. The difference lies, not in the methods used, but in the underlying nature of the research: carried out from a structural perspective to promote structural change. For example, for almost two decades a group called Campaign 2000 has been conducting research on child poverty in Canada. In 1989, the House of Commons unanimously adopted a resolution to eliminate child poverty in Canada by the year 2000. Every year, Campaign 2000, established on November 24, 1991, publishes the *Report Card on Child Poverty in Canada* to let the federal government know how it is doing in terms of meeting its promise. As you can imagine, the government has not achieved its goal. Nevertheless, the research conducted by Campaign 2000 serves as a constant reminder to the government to continue in its efforts. In 2009, on the twentieth anniversary of the adoption of the resolution, the government renewed its commitment to reduce and eventually eliminate child poverty in Canada. Our point here is that Campaign 2000 uses traditional quantitative methods of research, primarily data from Statistics Canada, with the goal of advocacy and creating change.

Another characteristic which sets structural data analysis apart from mainstream analysis is that the research is conducted as much as possible from an insider's perspective. As Linda Tuhiwai Smith (1999) explains, most research is conducted from the perspective of outsiders. The traditional positivist approach believes that researchers should be outsiders in the effort to remain neutral and objective. As stated many times in this book, research conducted from a structural perspective seeks maximum input from clients. Client participation in the analysis is as important as it is in the research design phase, as clients can provide invaluable information on the true meaning of the data.

There are several commonly used quantitative methods of data collection. Christine Marlow (2005) assesses the suitability of each by using neutrality and applicability as criteria. She uses the term "neutrality" instead of "objectivity," recognizing that objectivity is difficult to achieve even within the most rigorous of empirical studies. While we agree with Marlow that the term "objectivity" is problematic, we do not necessarily see "neutrality" as desirable. Because we believe that social work research should not be politically neutral, we prefer the term "objectivity," even with its drawbacks.

Interviews

The most common method of data collecting used in social work research is the interview; quantitative research uses structured interviews. The content of structured interviews is chosen before the data collection begins and is specific in terms of the information requested. Generally, all research participants are asked exactly the same questions in the same order using a rigid interview schedule. The interview can involve questions requesting numerical data, such as, "How many times have you used a given service?" or non-numerical data, such as, "Are you satisfied with a given service?" Usually the questions are closed or fixed-choice, where the researcher asks the participant to choose from a set of possible answers. Below are examples of closed questions, in this case taken from an online questionnaire exploring the service needs of LGBTTQ families. Participants are given a list of answers from which to choose their response.

2. What type(s) of family services do you currently access? (Check all that apply)

☐ Parenting courses
☐ Health services
☐ Counselling services
☐ Child care
☐ Educational
☐ Recreation
☐ Parent support groups
☐ Child/youth support groups
☐ Special/pride events
☐ Other: _____

3. Are there other services you do not currently access, but would like to access? (Check all that apply)

☐ Parenting courses
☐ Health services

☐ Counseling services
☐ Child care
☐ Educational
☐ Recreation
☐ Parent support groups
☐ Child/youth support groups
☐ Special/pride events
☐ Other: _____

4. How do you access services?

☐ Individually
☐ As a family
☐ Both[1]

In terms of the suitability of interviews as a data collecting method, it is difficult to achieve objectivity even with structured interviews. This is due to what Marlow (2005) calls the "reactive effect," which occurs when the interviewer somehow influences the responses of the interviewee. The classic example of the reactive effect was a series of studies done on worker productivity at the Hawthorne Plant of the Western Electric Company. When the lighting at the plant increased, productivity increased. However, when the lighting was later decreased, productivity did not fall. The conclusion was that productivity increased not because of the lighting but because of the extra attention workers were receiving. The term "The Hawthorne Effect" is still used to describe the impact on participants of being part of a study (Grinnell, Williams and Unrau 2011). The reactive effect is less of a concern with qualitative studies where it is recognized that a dynamic relationship exists between the interviewer and interviewee.

Another potential problem with any quantitative study, including interviews, is the response rate. While the response rate with interviews is often better than with other methods, if too many people refuse to participate in the interview, there may be sample bias. This is where the people who agree to participate feel differently about the topic than those who refuse. For instance, if the study is about client satisfaction with a program, clients who regard the program negatively may refuse to participate, even if confidentiality is assured. Methods used to increase response rate include incentives, such as food or coffee coupons. This practice of providing incentives is becoming more common as researchers acknowledge that participants are contributing their time and knowledge to the researcher. One of our research teams was sending questionnaires to a group of elderly participants and included a tea bag with their letter of information, which invited the potential participants to make themselves a cup of tea, relax and answer the survey. We thought this was a creative and inexpensive way to offer an incentive to participate.

With respect to applicability, interviews have advantages and disadvantages. On the positive side, they are usually better than other data collecting methods, such as anonymous surveys, in terms of the response rate. Interviews are also useful in dealing with participants who are not comfortable writing. On the negative side, besides the reactive effect, anonymity is an issue with face-to-face interviews as it is impossible to guarantee that others will not find out who has participated. This is less of a concern with phone interviews. Finally, costs associated with holding interviews, especially face-to-face, are higher than with other data collection methods.

Questionnaires

Another popular method of data collection is the questionnaire. The variety of types include the mailed questionnaire, including the increasingly popular electronic questionnaires, the face-to-face questionnaire, which is similar to face-to-face structured interviews, and group questionnaires, where a questionnaire is administered in a group setting. Each type has advantages and disadvantages.

Developing an effective questionnaire can be a daunting task. Peter Nardi (2003) offers the following steps to make this task more manageable. First, make a list of research questions. Next, develop an outline of what information is needed. This could include information on demographics, attitudes and behaviours. Demographic questions tell you who your participants are, questions on attitudes give you information on their opinions, and questions on behaviours tell you what they do. Each of these three areas could generate a list of questions. Carefully review your questions, adding what you believe is missing and deleting those that are redundant. Provide simple, clear instructions. Start with simple and routine questions and progress to more complex ones. Avoid "double barrelled" questions, which ask two things at the same time. Your questionnaire should be readable, using language that reflects the educational and reading levels of your participants. Finally, pre-test your questionnaire with people who are similar to your target population and ask them to tell you if any questions are unclear. Dudley provides the following useful examples of "flawed" questions:

> Questions with ambiguous wording:
> 1. What is your annual income?
> 2. When do you work?
> Two questions in one:
> 1. Do you think that the social worker was friendly and sensitive to your needs?

2. Are you satisfied with your supervisor, or would you prefer someone else?

Leading questions:

1. Do you support the woman's right to choose what happens to her body?
2. Do you support the right to life of a fetus?

Sensitive questions leading to normative responses:

1. Do you drive when you drink?
2. Do you beat your child?

Overlooking a timeframe:

1. Have you been dating anyone?
2. Are you satisfied with your school experience? (2010: 176)

In terms of objectivity, questionnaires tend to work better than interviews using open-ended questions as long as the questions are simple, clear and unambiguous (Marlow 2005). If participants are left wondering what is being asked, they will quickly lose interest. The response rate, especially with mailed questionnaires, tends to be very low, and sample bias is definitely a concern. The response rate is calculated by dividing the number of participants by the total number of questionnaires mailed. Although there is debate about what is a good response rate, many researchers consider that a response rate of at least 50 percent is adequate, 60 percent is good, and 70 percent is very good (Rubin and Babbie 2005). Nardi (2003: 111) states that response rates lower than 60 or 70 percent "may compromise the integrity of the random sample." The response rate of mailed questionnaires can be maximized by adding a letter describing the importance of the study. A follow-up letter would also encourage participants to respond (Marlow 2005), as will keeping the length of the questionnaire as short as possible. Finally, Christine Marlow suggests keeping the number of sensitive questions to a minimum and embedding them in the questionnaire. By starting with broad, general questions, a sense of comfort can be established, causing participants to be more willing to respond to sensitive questions.

The main advantage of mailed questionnaires is that they tend to be very cost effective and are also valuable if anonymity is important. But they can only be used with participants who are literate. The main disadvantage, as stated above, is that the response rate tends to be very low. If sample bias is a concern, other methods should be considered.

Observations

Another quantitative method is known as observation. Again, observations can be structured or unstructured. Structured observations are often used to measure specific behaviours. A good example is a parenting technique called a "token economy model," where the desired behaviour is rewarded using positive reinforcement, such as a sticker on a chart. This chart provides a quantitative record of the progress made by the child.

With respect to the objectivity of observations, structured observations will of course be more objective. For unstructured observations to be useful, researchers need extensive training. As Marlow (2005) cautions, the concern with unstructured observations is the reactive effect, this time upon the researcher, who may only record behaviours which support her thesis. This can be minimized by videotaping the behaviours for observation by a second researcher. This would provide inter-observer agreement (Yegidis and Weinbach 2009).

Looking at applicability, structured observations are useful in situations where the behaviours are clear and measurable. Unstructured observations are suitable if there is no specific target behaviour.

Secondary Data

Quantitative research often uses secondary data, which is data previously collected for another purpose. Large organizations often have extensive databases (for example, containing demographic client details) which could be used for a variety of purposes. A good example is the data collected by Statistic Canada, used extensively by policy analysts and activists alike.

In terms of objectivity, using data from organizations like Statistics Canada, which is viewed as objective, may lend credibility to a study. Straightforward demographic data that social service agencies have on file, such as clients' age, gender, ethnic origin, etc., is also considered objective. Other secondary data, such as case summaries and client assessments, are much less objective but may still provide valuable information. Other examples of less objective secondary data are newspaper articles and minutes of meetings, to name a couple. Sometimes researchers can create useful data for a quantitative study by converting non-numerical text into numerical data. An example would be counting the number of times a topic was discussed in an interview or during a meeting.

Secondary data, such as demographic data from agency files, is used extensively in social work research, for example, in program evaluations and needs assessments. Less objective data, such as newspaper articles or court proceedings, are used by social work researchers engaged in archival research. The important question is whether the secondary data being considered is appropriate for the study. As stated by Grinnell, Williams and Unrau (2011), the researcher cannot assume that the data collecting method was valid and reliable and is still responsible for verifying the data.

Scales

The last method considered here is the use of pre-existing standardized scales and tests. In research involving a more traditional positivist design, pre-existing instruments may be quite useful. The most known examples are IQ tests, but there are many other tests and scales, which are designed to measure such things as attitudes, levels of anxiety or depression, aptitudes, skills, client satisfaction, etc. While IQ tests have been criticized for being culturally biased, efforts are being made to make them less so. In our evaluation of a parenting program for Anishabe parents (van de Sande and Menzies 2003), a great deal of input was provided by Anishabe parents and workers in the creation of a culturally relevant scale.

Many of these instruments use a Likert scale, where participants are asked to rate particular questions on a five-point range, from, for instance, strongly agree to strongly disagree. If constructed according to specific guidelines and tested for reliability and validity, they it be an efficient way of gathering certain kinds of data. Several catalogues offering instruments for measuring a variety of traits are available online or through university libraries. The important considerations are whether the scales or tests actually measure the topic of interest of your study and whether they are appropriate for the population being studied.

Scales or tests, if tested for reliability and validity as stated above, are considered objective instruments by the traditional scientific community. Whether or not objectivity is possible or even desirable is something that needs to be decided when approaching your research. It is essential to weigh the advantages that come with using a standardized instrument versus the need to respect the diversity of the people being studied.

We suggest discussing the issue of using standardized data gathering instruments with client research partners. If the client and organizational members of the committee understand the concerns surrounding the use of standardized instruments and they want to proceed this way, researchers should be supportive of their wishes. The committee members may feel that using standardized instruments would establish "scientific" credibility with the outside world, which would outweigh the disadvantages. Will the means justify the ends, that is, the desired political and social ends?

Reliability and Validity

The test of reliability answers the question: "Does the instrument give the same information consistently over time?" The most common way of testing reliability is the test re-test method, where the same test is administered twice with a time interval in between. If the test re-test method is not possible or practical, another method is coefficient alpha, which is a computer-generated procedure used after the test has been administered to participants. The computer splits the test into two halves and compares results of one half with the other, and repeats this over and over again. The results are stated in terms of a correlation score, with 1.0 being the highest possible score. Any score of .8 or higher is considered acceptable (Yegidis and Weinbach 2009).

The test of validity answers the question: "Does this instrument measure what it intends to measure?" There are three types of validity tests. The most common is criterion validity, where the results of a new instrument are compared to the results of an existing instrument already confirmed to be valid (Marlow 2005). For instance, we could compare the client's self-reported level of depression with an existing standardized instrument measuring depression. The new instrument would require important advantages over the existing instrument, such as length or ease in administration, to be considered worthwhile. As with the test of reliability, the results are stated in terms of a correlation score, with any score over .8 considered acceptable.

Another common test is content validity (Marlow 2005) or face validity (Bryman and Teevan 2005), where the instrument is judged by recognized experts in the field. The example discussed earlier of the scale used to evaluate an Anishabe parenting program was developed using face validity. This method, while popular, is viewed as being more subjective than the test for criterion validity.

The last method is construct validity, where the instrument is tested against a theoretical construct (Marlow 2005). This is complicated and normally involves more advanced statistical tests such as factor analysis.

Organizing the Data

After the data has been collected it must be organized. As stated earlier, in quantitative research, decisions about categories and coding of the date have been made beforehand. For example, with questionnaires that involve closed questions, the data could be coded simply by counting the number of times participants checked each possible response.

Levels of Measurement

Organizing quantitative data depends in large part on the level of measurement used (Weinbach and Grinnell 2007). There are four levels of measurement: nominal, ordinal, interval and ratio. Nominal level measurement involves classifying observations into mutually exclusive categories, such as sex: male or female. The ordinal level is used when classifying observations that are mutually exclusive and have an inherent order to them, for example, level of education: elementary school, high school or university. The interval level involves classifying observations that are mutually exclusive, have an inherent order and are equally spaced, as in the job satisfaction survey shown in Table 11-1.

Table 11-1 Example of Ordinal Data: Job Satisfaction Survey

	Job Satisfaction Questionnaire	
	In the column on the right marked "score," please indicate the extent to which you agree or disagree with the statements below using the following scale. 1. Strongly disagree 2. Disagree 3. No Opinion 4. Agree 5. Strongly Agree	
Item	Statements	score
1	I receive a fair wage for my job.	
2	I have adequate benefits for health and dental.	
3	There is a reasonable pension program.	
4	I receive adequate time for vacations.	
5	I receive positive recognition for the work I do.	
6	My supervisor is supportive of the work I do.	
7	My work is stimulating.	
8	There adequate opportunities for advancement.	
9	My workplace environment is safe and supportive.	
10	I am able to take time off to care for a sick relative.	
	Total	

The highest level of measurement is the ratio level, which is used when classifying observations that are mutually exclusive, have an inherent order, are equally spaced and reflect the absolute minimum, zero. A typical example is income.

The reason why distinguishing the different levels is important is that statistical tests require certain levels of data (discussed further below). While some research studies can only produce nominal level data, researchers strive to use the highest and most precise level possible in a given research situation (see Table 11-2 for a breakdown of measurement levels).

Table 11-2 Levels of Measurement

Level	Numerical Value Requirements
Nominal	None: uses value categories
Ordinal	Values must preserve rank order
Interval	Values must preserve rank order and unit difference
Ratio	Values must preserve rank order, unit difference and have a fixed zero point

Codes

The first step in transferring information from the questionnaire into a form that can be analyzed involves organizing the data into codes. This requires the following three steps:

1. converting the responses to numerical codes;
2. assigning names to variables; and
3. creating a code book.

Converting the Responses to Numerical Codes

Coding the responses from participants depends on the wording of the question and the different possible responses. For instance, for questions such as, "How many months have you received service?" the answer is a simple and obvious numerical response. This would be ratio level data. On the other hand, questions such as, "How satisfied are you with the service?" where we provided a range of possible responses including very dissatisfied, dissatisfied, no opinion, satisfied and very satisfied, require that we assign a number to each category (e.g., one for very dissatisfied and five for very satisfied). This is called ordinal level data. If we ask respondents to specify which service they receive out of four possible services (such as individual counselling, group counselling, family counselling and crisis intervention) and we ask respondents to check all that apply, each service would be coded separately. We might code each service as one for used and two for not used. This is called nominal level data. Finally, if we provide a category called '"other" and we receive responses such as employment counselling or financial advising, we could create new categories for each different answer, or we may feel that these responses fit into a pre-existing category, e.g., individual counselling (Marlow 2005).

Whatever the type of question, the coding categories should be mutually exclusive and exhaustive (Marlow 2005). By mutually exclusive, we mean that each response should only be able to fit into one category. By exhaustive, we mean that all possible responses fit in the categories. Again, responses that do not fit into existing categories could be dealt with by creating new categories or fitting them into existing categories.

Assigning Names to Variables

The names of the variables should be relatively short for ease of manipulation and recording, and because most statistical computer software programs demand short labels. So a question like "How satisfied are you?" could be labelled Satisfy. For the three types of service, the labels could be Individual, Group and Family.

Creating a Code Book

The code book tells other researchers the variable names and values. For example, for the variable "satisfaction with the program," the name of the variable could be Satisfy, and the values could range from one, to indicate very dissatisfied, to five, for very satisfied.

Computer Software for Organizing Data

A number of software packages are available to help organize and analyze quantitative data. One of the most popular is SPSS (Statistical Package for the Social Sciences).

Descriptive Statistics

Quantitative statistical analysis is normally divided into two large categories: descriptive and inferential. Descriptive statistics describe the characteristics of a group of people. To describe a typical case in our population, we would use measures of central tendency, the three common measures of which are mode, median and mean. The mode is the value that appears most often, the median is the half-way point between the range of values, and the mean is the average of all the values. To describe the range of values, the most common method is the standard deviation, which describes the average distance of all the values from the mean (Weinbach and Grinnell 2007).

Most research projects, particularly those carried out by students, involve descriptive analysis. In the case of needs assessments, the data analysis can be presented using frequency tables, bar charts and graphs that describe the characteristics and needs of the clients. In the case of client satisfaction surveys, the analysis would result in frequency tables indicating the percentage of clients who are satisfied with the program. For example, if the scale provides a range of responses from one being poor to four being excellent, a frequency table could show how many clients checked off the various levels of satisfaction, as in the following example.

1) Poor	2) Fair	3) Good	4) Excellent
3	7	12	8

Inferential Statistics

Inferential statistics are used when we want to generalize our findings to a larger population based on a sample of cases. If the sample has been selected using a probability approach, meaning that each individual within the population of interest had an equal chance of being selected, then we can infer the characteristics of the population from the characteristics of our sample (Weinbach and Grinnell 2007). For instance, if an agency has a total caseload of 1000 clients, we could randomly select a sample of 100 for our study, and, as long as the characteristics of the sample are similar to the total client population, we can infer that the results are applicable to the entire client population.

We might also want to find out if there is a relationship between two or more variables. For instance, in the case of a summative program evaluation, we would use an explanatory approach, which will tell us if there is a cause-and-effect relationship between the program (the causal or independent variable) and the effect on clients (the dependent variable). For example, we want to demonstrate that a program designed to help clients raise their self-esteem is effective. If we use a classic experimental design with a control group, we will be able to compare the scores obtained by the experimental group with those obtained by the control group. We would start with a hypothesis, which is a testable statement describing the relationship between the independent and dependent variables. For example: "Participants in the self-esteem group will score higher than participants on the control group." For this type of analysis we would use the t test. The t test is a parametric test that requires data for the dependent (outcome) variable, such as self-esteem scores, to be at the interval or ratio level.

On the other hand, if we are only able to obtain data at the nominal level, we can still carry out a program evaluation using a test such as the chi-square test. Let's say we are looking at a program to help women survivors of abuse become more assertive, and we want to know if women who attend the program are less likely to return to abusive situations. We would still have two variables. The independent variable would be the program, and the data would be at the nominal level, with two possible scores: attend or did not attend. The data for the dependent or outcome variable would also be at the nominal level, with two scores: return or did not return to an abusive situation. While this type of study would not establish a cause-and-effect relationship, we could state that there is a relationship between attending the program and not returning to an abusive situation.

Another typical statistical test is called correlation. In considering a hypothetical study of child protection workers and job satisfaction, we could see if there is a relationship between years of service and job satisfaction. Knowing that here is a high turnover in child protection work, our research question would be: "Is there a relationship between length of employment in child protection work and the level of job satisfaction?" This test requires that the data for both variables be at the interval or ratio level.

This chapter covers some of the main points of a quantitative research approach. Students are encouraged to consult the increasing number and variety of social work research texts that cover the subject in more detail. A word of caution: all texts have a certain bias, just as our does. Therefore, read texts critically to determine if they adequately address the issue of diversity and respect structural and anti-oppressive principles.

DISCUSSION QUESTIONS

1. Do you believe that a quantitative design is inconsistent with a structural and anti-oppressive approach to research? Explain.
2. Can you provide an example of how a positivist and empiricist orientation can be used for social change?
3. What are the challenges in using a quantitative design with a PAR approach?
4. Where do you stand with respect to the quantitative versus qualitative debate?

Note

1. Shannon Sommerauer, Kate Hanton, Shellie Bird, "Around the Rainbow Project Report," March 31, 2010.

12. Report Writing

After the data collection and analysis have been completed, it is time to write the final research report. Traditional scientific writing follows specific guidelines. Those of us who took social work research courses before the 1980s were told, for example, that our reports had to be written in the third person passive rather than the first person active. In other words, we were required to use phrases such as "It was found" rather than "We found that" in order to maintain the appearance of objectivity and neutrality.

However, as a result of the influence of post-modernism and the feminist critique of traditional science, there are now a range of possible approaches to writing. While the traditional approach is still required in many circles, such as the natural sciences and some social sciences, using the first person active is now accepted and, in the case of the interpretivist approach, expected. This form of writing acknowledges that complete objectivity and neutrality are not possible and that you cannot separate the researcher from the research.

As social work researchers operating from a structural social work perspective, our first concern is the people we serve. We want to ensure that our research is useful to the people who are the focus of our research. We may, nevertheless, be obliged to write in a traditional academic format if the report will be presented to an academic or government audience, for example, if our research partners or advisory committee feel this is the appropriate route to take.

In order to share the research results with service user research partners, the report should be written in language that is accessible to these partners. Regardless of the style, keep in mind that the ultimate goal of our research is structural change and the elimination of oppression. It is important to identify our audience. Since one of the goals of community-based research is social action and social change, the report might look and sound different in order to instigate that change. Some community-based research projects use "photovoice," which involves research participants taking photographs of certain aspects of their lives. The final report could involve a photo exhibit or a book of photographs taken by the participants. Bruce Berg (2004) supplies an example where fifteen adolescents were given cameras and asked to capture photographs of their urban community. These photographs of their friends, family, neighbours, and where they lived, played and went to school were shown in three exhibits, to which the youth invited community members. This kind of presentation can be used to begin a discussion about community needs, highlight dangerous places for youth and document the lack of recreational facilities or whatever social issue the community wants to pursue.

Increasingly, social work researchers have to write two reports, a formal one for an academic and/or government audience and a more user-friendly version for client research partners. Our graduate students are often asked to prepare a Powerpoint presentation in plain, non-academic language for community members in addition to the formal report for the agency requesting the research. At times, an executive summary with bullets outlining the most salient research results is all that some community agencies require. A study involving qualitative research might include 1) an overview of the project, including the research question; 2) thematic findings from the literature; 3) thematic findings from the research; 4) ideas for future research; and 5) implications for the agency or social work. The following is an example of an executive summary for a study of best practices in an anti-violence program:

Executive Summary

From September until March, a research project was conducted entitled 'Best Practices Review of the Anti-Violence Program.' The purpose of the project was to conduct an extensive literature review and to interview program facilitators regarding the implementation of practices and techniques. During the project, the pool of potential participants was expanded to include members of the steering committee. The qualitative research suggests that a number of the aspects of the program are in keeping with the best practices found in the literature, such as: providing group and individual counseling, including a mentorship element (the friend line), a psycho-educational component, facilitating the connection to community resources, and grouping participants by age and gender. A summary of the research follows.

Best Practices as Identified in the Literature
• Group youth according to developmental stage
• Group youth according to gender
• Explicitly address race and ethnicity
• Program success is influenced by the level of education and experience of the facilitators
• Combination of individual and group counseling
• Need for positive connections between family, school and community

- A therapeutic framework
- Effective program evaluation

Results from the Research

Program Components:
- Facilitators have about 10 years of experience and all have related education.
- There is considerable ethno-cultural and socio-economic diversity of the program.
- Participants are predominantly male.

Strengths of the Program:
- Value in the friend line
- Value of connecting youth to community resources
- The use of eclectic approaches (narrative, solution-focused, etc)
- Flexibility of offering both individual and group counseling

Areas for Improvement:
- Need for consistent funding
- Need to make the program more inclusive (francophone, girls, school-based, geographical)
- Expand facilitator training[1]

The following are questions to ask yourself in relation to the audience of the report:

- What do the various research partners want to know and why? What expectations do they have for the report?
- Will the research participants be making decisions about policies, programs or practices based on the findings of the report? If so, what decisions?
- Are there any ethical or political considerations that need to be carefully thought out before preparing the report? Are there any controversial issues that need to be addressed in a manner that is most advantageous to the social justice goals of the research?
- How do service users benefit from the findings? How do service users use this information and in what form to help them maximize the benefit?

Contemporary Writing Issues

As stated above, post-modernism has challenged the claim that there is only one correct style of presenting research. Laurel Richardson explains that academic disciplines have been affected by the "post-modern critique of what constitutes knowledge, and how and for whom knowledge is created" (1990: 11). Historically, dating back to the seventeenth century, writing was divided into two main categories, literary and scientific. Literary writing was viewed as subjective and focused on such values as aesthetics, ethics, morality and humanity. Scientific writing, on the other hand, was seen as objective, precise and unambiguous (Richardson 1990).

Since the 1970s, feminist scholars, in particular, but others as well, have challenged ideas about what constitutes acceptable scientific writing, putting forth a number of important criticisms of traditional science. First, they argued that one cannot separate science from the social context in which it is conducted, because in reality, science is a social endeavour (Letherby 2003). Next, they insisted that science is not neutral or value free because values cannot be turned on or off like a switch (Letherby 2003). Finally, they urged researchers to acknowledge their location in the research report, including documenting their values and emotions (Letherby 2003; Harding 1987). The example we presented in the chapter on program evaluation illustrates these issues. LEAP was a provincially funded program that provided support to young mothers. Evaluating that program could be done from different value perspectives. The goal of the provincial government was to educate young, single mothers so that they could be more employable, return to the labour force and get off welfare. If the evaluator held the same neoliberal value perspective, the main indicator of the success of the program would be how many young moms got off of welfare and secured full-time employment. The municipal government, which provided the services, saw this provincial funding as an opportunity to help young single moms in numerous ways and supplemented what the province provided. For example, the municipality supplied proms dresses, which can be out of reach for someone on a tight budget, for the students who graduated from high school. The city workers wanted these young moms to have as normal a graduation experience as possible. Such actions represent values of compassion and empowerment. The researcher was operating from a feminist perspective and saw the program as coercive and representative of a patriarchal system. The municipal government was concerned about what was reported, in particular the risk of losing future funding if the provincial authorities discovered it had supplemented the program funding. The researcher worked in concert with the municipal research partners to include her analysis but be cognizant of their fears. While modernism and positivism continue to be the dominant scientific paradigm in our society, certainly in social work, post-modernism and the interpretivist approach to writing research reports are making many inroads.

The Writing Process

One of the goals of community-based research is social action and social change. This can be reflected in the writing process and report (see Figure 10-1, reproduced from Chapter Four).

Figure 10-1 The Process of Community-Based Research

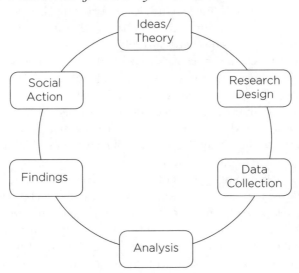

All aspects of the research feed into each other. Ideas and theory give rise to the design, which influences the data collection, which guides the analysis, which directs the findings, which contribute to social action, which gives rise to new ideas and theories. The report can reflect this research cycle. Christine Marlow (2005) offers the following useful tips to make the writing process as painless as possible. Following them can save much time and frustration later on.

1. Keep a log for ideas and decisions taken along the way.
2. Prepare an outline; the more detail the easier the final report will be.
3. Write a first draft. This is often the hardest part. Revise several times if necessary.
4. Ask a colleague, your research partners or advisory committee members to proof the draft and do not be afraid of criticism. The more input, the higher the quality.
5. Have someone proof the final copy. There are usually mistakes that you will miss.

Traditional Scientific Format

The traditional academic format normally includes the following sections: title page; abstract; introduction; literature review; methodology; findings; discussion; conclusion; bibliography; and appendices.

Title Page

In addition to the usual details such as the date and list of authors with their degrees, the title page provides the reader with enough information without being overly wordy. Try to come up with a title that will catch the reader's interest. However, as Allan Rubin and Earl Babbie (2008) point out, for a formal academic report, you do not want to come across as unscholarly. Achieving the right balance is not always simple, and it would be wise to seek feedback from colleagues.

Abstract

The abstract is a brief summary of the research. Seventy-five to 150 words is often plenty, but it can be as long as 200 words. Include information on the purpose of the study, the research question or questions and the central thesis. It should have a line or two on the research design or methodology and conclude with a couple of sentences on the major findings and their implications for social work practice. If you are hoping to present your research at an academic or professional conference, the abstract is what you submit to the organizers along with your application.

Introduction

The introduction is the first part of the main body of the report and provides the background to the study. Include the scope of the problem being investigated, the goals and objectives of the research, the specific research question or questions and the theory that has informed your research. If your study follows a traditional empirical design, also include your research hypothesis and the conceptualization and operationalization of the variables. The conceptualization of the variables provides the reader with clear and specific definitions of each of the variables, both the independent or causal variable and the dependent or outcome variable. The operationalization explains how these variables have been measured.

Literature Review

The literature review is essentially a summary of what has already been written on the topic of your investigation. It is important to present a conscientious review of the literature, including a historical summary as well as current theoretical or scholarly research related to your topic. If studies on your topic give contradictory views, provide a brief overview of the various sides of the question. If you disagree with what the literature says, provide an argument for your position. End the literature review with a statement about the gaps in knowledge and how your research attempts to fill these gaps. Below is an example of how a literature review might begin:

> The Keeping it Cool program (KIC) is an anti-violence and anger management program for boys and girls ranging in age from 12

to 18. Therefore, the literature search using the psychINFO database included the keywords (in various combinations): youth, adolescent, boys, girls, anger management, and anti-violence. Based on preliminary searches, the use of these keywords yielded 204 potential articles from peer review journals. The titles of these articles were critiqued for inclusion, and when in doubt, the abstracts were consulted. This narrowed the potential articles to 54. The abstracts were then consulted and the articles skimmed for relevance.[2]

Methodology

The methodology of a traditional academic report includes a number of sub-sections, such as participant selection, measurement instruments, identification variables, both independent and dependent, measurement procedures and statistical methods of analysis. In describing the selection of participants, explain how participants were contacted and whether you used a probability sampling method, such as a simple random sample, or a non-probability sampling method, such as convenience or availability. If you used a standardized measurement instrument, include the reliability and validity scores. Finally, state which statistical test you used and whether it was a parametric test, such as a t-test, or non-parametric test, such as chi square test. It is also important to note that your research was reviewed and approved by a university or community ethics review committee.

Findings

The findings section in a traditional research report contains the results of the investigation. With a quantitative design, this section includes tables and graphs. Also state if the results were statistically significant and whether or not they supported your research hypothesis. Including tables is a good way to summarize the data and present it visually. It is important to give the table a clear and descriptive title. The reader should be able to look at the title and the table and understand what it is trying to say without reading the text. Order the tables to highlight important points. Finally, to make the table accurate, include the number of cases on which the percentages are based and round the percentages to the nearest whole number.

Discussion and Conclusion

In the discussion and conclusion section, relate the results of your investigation back to the literature review. Do your results support or contradict the literature? What are the implications of your research for social work practice and how have the results added to the knowledge on the topic of your investigation? The discussion should also include a sub-section on limitations. With every study, no matter how well designed, there are always some external variables affecting the results. Maybe the response rate was less than expected, resulting in some sample bias. Maybe there were problems with the administration of the instrument, resulting in some design error. Finally, in order to help other researchers interested in the same topic, end this section with suggestions for further research.

Bibliography

The bibliographies of most social science reports follow the APA (American Psychological Association) method of referencing. It is important that your bibliography provide complete and accurate information on all your sources. Your credibility will be questioned if information is missing or there are errors in formatting.

Appendices

The appendix section of your report should include, as a minimum, the measurement instrument used and copies of ethical consent letters. Many researchers provide additional results — tables that were not included in the findings section but may still be useful to the readers. Each appendix should be clearly labelled using letters (A, B, C, etc.).

The Interpretivist Format

Unlike the traditional scientific format presented above, there is no standard format for the interpretivist approach. The important factors to remember are that the writing process includes consultation with and feedback from the research partners and that the report is accessible to research participants and other community members. In this section, we use the terms interpretivist and qualitative interchangeably. As Tutty, Rothery and Grinnell (1996) explain, the form and style of a qualitative report depends largely on the intended audience. They mention that qualitative reports often look like books because the book format lends itself to narrative report writing that is rich in detail.

Before you begin to write, there are a few things to keep in mind. Tutty, Rothery and Grinnell (1996) offer the following useful suggestions. First, avoid trying to write up a qualitative study using quantitative terminology. In terms of demonstrating rigour, in quantitative reports we discuss concepts such as reliability and validity, whereas in qualitative reports, we refer to trustworthiness. Establishing trustworthiness in qualitative studies can be done by reporting on techniques, such as maintaining detailed case records, using triangulation and peer debriefing, analyzing negative cases, where you revise your analysis until you account for all cases, and member checking, where you ask participants to provide feedback on your conclusions.

Be very mindful of your writing style. Interpretivist reports are written in the first person active, acknowledging the researcher's participation in the research. Thoughts and impressions are important aspects of this research. Your reactions to the content of interviews provide insight into interviewer/ interviewee dynamics. Frequent quotes can be used for illustrating the interpretation and conclusions. This is usually done in consultation with the research partners or advisory committee. Finally, choose an outline for your report. Here again, there is quite a range of acceptable formats. We present a form suggested by Bruce Berg (2007) and include comments from Tutty, Rothery and Grinnell (1996), pointing out the similarities to and differences from the quantitative format.

Title Page
Just as is the case with the traditional format, the title of the report should give the reader a good idea of what the study is about. You want to catch the reader's attention without being "too cute or whimsical" (Berg 2007: 348).

Abstract
The abstract used for qualitative studies is similar to that for quantitative reports. Include a brief overview of the project, including your research methodology, findings and recommendations (see following example):

> Rainbow Families Research Project conducted a demographic profile and needs assessment of Lesbian, Gay, Bisexual, Trans, Two-Spirit and Queer (LGBTTQ) families in the Ottawa region. LGBTTQ family members and service providers were invited to complete an anonymous online survey to provide feedback on a variety of issues related to the provision of social services.

> The study found that LGBTTQ families continue to face pervasive discrimination from institutions and social service agencies. Based on the results of our study, it is recommended that the following needs be addressed:

> 1. Specialized training for service providers in anti-oppressive practice with LGBTTQ families.
> 2. Further community development initiatives and outreach for LGBTTQ families.
> 3. The establishment of more inclusive and accepting services for trans people.
> 4. The development of more specialized parenting courses, youth groups, counselling services and recreational events.
> 5. Further research to determine the most effective training strategies to increase service provider knowledge, and reduce heterosexism and discrimination within XXXX's institutions and social service agencies. Further research on the experiences of LGBTTQ family members who identify as trans, two-spirit, members of a visible minority and people whose first language is other than English, is also suggested.[3]

Introduction
The introduction section is also similar to the traditional format. Provide a background to the study along with the research question or questions and

the theoretical framework. Berg (2007) describes the introduction as a map of the report, helping the reader situate the study in its historical and theoretical context. While Tutty, Rothery and Grinnell (1996) suggest combining the introduction with the literature review, Berg states that these two sections can be kept separate.

Either in the introduction or a separate section, many feminist and community-based researchers articulate their location and reasons for engaging in the research. Janice Ristock and Joan Pennell (1996) explain how and why they do so:

> Articulating a reflexive analysis and exploring our own subjectivities and locations as researchers are necessary in order to bring forward questions of accountability such as 'Why am I doing this research?' and 'Who am I doing it for?' What I conclude is that feminist researchers are correct in noting that our identities, locations, and experiences do shape our work. My history as a lesbian will inevitably inform my research (just as a straight woman's will inform hers) even when it does not seem central to the topic. (76)

Literature Review

The literature review described by Berg parallels those found in quantitative studies and serves a similar function. Berg adds that there is a hierarchy of credibility when it comes to reference sources. Interestingly enough, at the top of his list are scholarly "empirical" articles. This list would obviously apply to quantitative studies as well, evidence that the positivist paradigm continues to influence our research. The format of the literature review depends on your audience. If you are producing an executive summary for a community group or agency, the literature review does not have to and probably should not follow the traditional, X said, Y said, Z said format. Rather, it can be a discussion or bullet points referring to the issues raised in the literature and the various ways those issues have been conceptualized and argued elsewhere. Include the writing of scholars — community-based research does not have to be anti-intellectual. This can be very helpful in setting the context of the particular research.

Methodology

The methodology section in qualitative research reports describes how the research was conducted, just as it does in quantitative reports. It is important to discuss how the participants were recruited, what sampling techniques you utilized and the rational for your sampling technique. The most common sampling techniques used in community-based research are purposive sampling, deliberately choosing a group of people to participate in your study; convenience sampling, choosing participants because they are readily available; and snowball sampling, asking participants to identify other people they know who might be interested in being involved in the study. For example, a study mentioned before explored the benefits to mental health service users of participating in service-user businesses. Since there are few service-user businesses in most cities, the pool of potential participants is small. The research partners decided to use purposive sampling and try to recruit as many people working in those businesses of the clients as possible. In another study discussed previously involving sex trade workers, the research team used the snowball approach. They identified sex trade workers they knew and asked them to participate. They were in turn asked to talk to their friends about the project and see if other participants would come forward.

It is important to provide a rationale for your chosen data gathering method — interviews, focus groups, etc. If you used an interview guide, it is helpful to explain how it was developed, what role the various research participants or advisory committee played, how you chose your questions and how it was pre-tested. Below is an example of how to explain the role the advisory committee played in developing the research instrument.

> In designing the survey, research team members incorporated a number of consultation processes, including consultation with our advisory committee made up of fellow research students, Family Services (FS) and the Around the Rainbow Project. Feedback on the wording and design of questions was incorporated in the final survey. This process allowed us to utilize the experience of fellow students and of the Rainbow Family Coalition and FS in working with the LGBTTQ community. In this way, we also worked to mitigate researcher bias in the survey design.[4]

Tutty, Rothery and Grinnell (1996) add that here is where you should describe the techniques you used to establish trustworthiness. This includes the trustworthiness of the research process, which we discussed in the chapter on qualitative research, and how the trust of the community and research partners was gained and maintained. The latter aspect we discussed in the chapters on research partners and Aboriginal research. It is important to note that your research was reviewed and approved by a university or community ethics review committee.

Findings and Discussion
In most qualitative studies, the findings and discussion sections are combined. Provide descriptive profiles of your participants along with frequent quotes that provide evidence for your conclusions and illustrate the questions you are exploring (Tutty, Rothery and Grinnell 1996). In your descriptive profiles, make sure that you leave out information that could readily identify the participants to community members who read the final report. This involves

giving the participants a pseudonym. It is also typical to relate your findings to the literature and indicate whether your findings confirm or contradict what others have found. Your findings should be organized in relation to the themes you identify from the data analysis, discussed in Chapter Ten. Your findings can be used to support or contradict theories that exist in the literature. They can also be used in political or policy statements to support social action. Appendix 5 includes an example of how to write about your findings from a study of the service needs of LGBTTQ families.

Conclusions

In qualitative research reports, the conclusion provides the authors with space to describe what they believe to be the significance of the study. Tutty, Rothery and Grinnell (1996) explain that an interpretive research study should begin and end with the writer. While the results of a qualitative study are not statistically generalizable to a wider population, the author should attempt to reach a balance between not generalizing and still describing the potential significance of the study to similar populations. In terms of the bibliography, there are no differences between qualitative and quantitative reports. Both primarily use the APA format. The appendices section is also similar with both approaches.

Take Action!

Writing and disseminating the report are very exciting parts of the research process. As the community-based research cycle shows (see Figure 4-1 in Chapter Four), we have now come full circle. After analyzing your findings and disseminating the report, the next part of the research cycle includes using your research for social action. Present your findings at a community meeting and get people excited about organizing to change the problem you have documented. Present your findings at a city council meeting and convince counsellors that the community you are working with needs extra resources to tackle some of these difficulties. Take action!

DISCUSSION QUESTIONS

1. What are some of the challenges in writing an academic research paper for a lay audience?
2. How important is it to maintain academic rigour in a report prepared for a mainstream audience?
3. How do you feel about writing a research report in the third person passive versus the first person active?
4. In using a PAR approach, how much input should research participants have in the writing of the final report?

Notes

1. Best Practices Review of Anti-Violence Program Executive Summary by Chantelle Carrier, Krista Hall, Honora Harvey and Marie Perry (2011).

2. Ibid.
3. Shannon Sommerauer, Kate Hanton, Shellie Bird, *Around the Rainbow Project Report*, Student research project, Carleton University, March 31, 2010.
4 Ibid.

Appendix 1

Example of a Letter Advertising an Upcoming Research Project

Dear participant,

We want to hear from you!

The (name of agency and name of department) students invite you to take part in a research study on the (agency) services. The research team has created a questionnaire that will help to find out the personal impact that using (agency) services has had on the lives of clients at least six months after they have finished their program.

The research team will be giving out the questionnaires during a series of drop-in evenings that will be held between December 2010 and February 2011. Please carefully read through the information below for more details about the study. Please ask a member of the research team if you have any questions about the study.

Important Information
- The questionnaire has 35 short questions and will take about 15–20 minutes to fill out.
- Your participation in the study may be known by other participants or staff.
- However, your answers will be completely anonymous. You do not need to add your name to the questionnaire and there will be no questions that could identify you.
- You are asked to complete the questionnaire and then seal your answers in an unmarked (department) envelope.
- Your participation is entirely your choice and if you decide to end your participation in the study, you may do so up until you hand in your questionnaire.
- You can choose not to answer certain questions without consequences. We realize that some questions are more sensitive than others, and that you may feel uncomfortable answering them.
- Your decision to participate or not will not affect your ability to access (agency) programs or services in the future.

Please keep in mind
- Your answers will be kept confidential and under the control of the research team.
- Only the research team will be administering the questionnaires and

will have access to completed questionnaires.

- All completed questionnaires will be kept under lock and key at (department) until the project is finished and will then be destroyed.
- The results from this study will be presented to (agency) staff in March 2011, and will be made available to participants and the general public upon request.
- If you wish to fill out a questionnaire, please sign the consent section at the end of this letter. You must sign your consent in order to take part in the study.
- If you have any other concerns or questions about being part of this study, you may also contact (name) at the contact below.
- If you have experienced any negative feelings from filling out the questionnaire and feel that you would like to talk to an experienced counselor, please call (agency) at (number). If you need to speak to someone immediately, please call the crisis line at (number).

If you feel you may need some help in filling out the questionnaire, please ask a member of the research team. Please note that we are bound by the limits of confidentiality. This means, if you tell us that you intend to harm yourself or someone else, or if you report abuse of anyone under the age of 16, we have to report these instances to the authorities.

To thank you for your participation, food and beverages will be provided![1]

Source: Chandni Desai, Leigh Hortop, Julia Hunt, Matthew Manion, Lee Ann McGuire, Letter of information from their research project, 2010.

Example of a Typical Consent Form

Title of Research Project:
Community Engagement in Ottawa Housing

Date of ethics clearance: To be determined
Ethics clearance for data collection expires: May 31, 2011

Dear Mr./Ms.,

You are invited to participate in a study that will investigate engagement in social housing communities. The study will be conducted by three Master of Social Work students, under the supervision of Professor XX at the University. The purpose of this letter is to inform you of the purpose, procedures, benefits, risks, participation, privacy and use of data so that you can decide whether or not you want to participate in the study.

Purpose

You have been invited to participate in the study because you were identified as someone who organizes community events, by the Community Coordinator and/or another research participant. The study will help the Ottawa Coalition of Community Houses understand how to best support you and other community organizers. The researchers seek your assistance to help us better understand your perspectives as a community organizer.

Procedure

If you choose to participate in this study, you will be invited to attend one focus group which will be a discussion with five to eight other organizers within your community. The focus group will be held at your Community House and will take about 60 to 90 minutes of your time. The researchers may ask what motivated you to become involved in your community, what has sustained your involvement, what are barriers or challenges to involvement and how can the Community House support you and other community organizers?

The focus group will not be recorded on audio or videotape. One researcher will conduct the conversation and two other researchers will record notes during the focus group. A blank form with a self-addressed, stamped envelope will be provided at the end of the focus group for you to submit additional comments, at your choice. The blank form is an opportunity to provide information for the study that you did not feel comfortable to share during the focus group.

Benefits

You may benefit from the focus group by sharing and learning about challenges and ideas that are useful for community involvement. You will have an opportunity to discuss how you want to be supported in your role. The results from the study will be provided to the Ottawa Coalition of Community Houses and other community members to learn ways to better support you as an organizer and to also encourage involvement from other persons in the community. To assist with your participation in the study, childcare will be provided during the focus groups. The researchers can seek translators or interpreters for participants, as needed.

Risks

You may feel discomfort if you discuss personal or sensitive information. Comments or information shared during the focus group have the potential to be upsetting. You may also be concerned with loss of privacy because other participants may be your neighbours and/or other community members. The researchers hope to limit the possibility of feeling uncomfortable in the group. At the beginning of the discussion, the researchers will create ground rules with the group for the discussion and will also ask that participants try to avoid comments that may be hurtful to other participants. If you feel discomfort as a result of the focus group and would like to seek support, you can contact the Ottawa Distress Line.

Voluntary Participation

Participation in the study is voluntary. You do not have to answer any questions in the focus group that make you feel uncomfortable. You may leave the focus group at any time and will not need to explain why you have changed your mind. We will not be able to withdraw your contributions to the study after the focus group because a focus group depends on a discussion where participants build upon each other's comments. The blank form and stamped envelope will be the opportunity for you to add, clarify or request certain statements to not be included in data analysis. We ask that participants submit the form in the envelope within two days after the focus group to allow the participants to gather the information in time for data analysis.

Privacy

Due to the nature of a focus group, we cannot fully protect confidentiality or privacy for the information you share in the discussion. We cannot guarantee that other participants will not disclose information learned during the focus group.

After the focus group we, the researchers, will be the only persons who have access to the research data, including the notes taken during the focus group. Information collected during the study will be stored in a locked office at the School of Social Work and on a password protected flash drive, until the final research paper is complete. Exceptions to information about the data are that the researchers are legally required to report if they hear of anyone stating knowledge of harm to a child, themselves or another person.

We can offer limited confidentiality for the final report of the study. The final report will not include your name or any other identifying information about you. Findings from three focus groups in different housing communities will be integrated. The data will be destroyed by May 31, 2011. All paper records will be shredded and all documents on the flash drive will be deleted.

Use of Data

Findings will be shared with research supervisors, students and with the Ottawa Coalition of Community Houses. We will invite participants, including you, community members, the Ottawa Coalition of Community Houses and Ottawa Community Housing to a presentation on the research findings. The findings may also be presented at other workshops, conferences or in other academic literature. The final report will be available to the participants and will be held at the participating Community Houses.

Questions

If you have any questions prior to the focus group, please contact the researchers. You may confirm the ethical approval of this study or raise concerns you may have, by contacting the University Research Ethics Board. Contact information for the researchers, research supervisor and the Research Ethics Board is listed on the next page.

Consent Section

The researchers want to ensure that you have fully understood the risks, benefits and procedures of the study as outlined in this form. We want you to feel comfortable that all of your questions about the study have been answered to your satisfaction. You will give consent to participate in this study by joining and staying in the focus group session.

Additional Contact Information

The Research Team
Chair Research Ethics Board

If you understand the conditions in this form and agree to participate in the study, please sign below.

Signature of Participant: _____ Date: _____
Signature of Researcher: _____ Date: _____

Source: Christine Howey, Elizabeth Whyte and Mike Garbutt, Recruitment document, student research project, Carleton University, 2011.

Appendix 3

Typical University-Based Research Ethics Application

Ethics Application   Research Ethics Board

Application for Ethics Approval for Human Participant Research

SECTION 1: General Information
☐ Individual project   ☐ Group project

1. Researcher information: (If applicable, provide names and contact information for all members of research team)
Supervisor information:

2. Title of Research Project: Rainbow Families Research Project

3. Research Dates:
Start date:
Expected date of completion:

4. Agency participation:
Will an agency play an active role in the project? ☐Yes   ☐ No
If you answered **yes**, please explain that role in detail (50 words).

> Family Services will lead this research project, working with their partners. Through regular meetings with FS staff, the student research team will develop research project materials, communications flyer and outreach. They will work closely with the research team to develop the survey questions, direct potential participants to the survey, and outreach through their own and other community networks to promote the project. They will also supervise data collection and analysis, up to and including the report on the research findings.

5. Letter of support from agency, NGO or other institution:
☐ Not applicable   ☐ Letter secured (copy attached)

6. Contact name and information for agency:

7. Location(s) where the research will be conducted:

> The research survey will be made available on-line through

local agency web sites (see attached list) and as a Facebook campaign and Twitter

8. Additional reviews: *Final approval may depend upon approval by another review board. Indicate all other reviews and approvals required before the research can begin. If the University approval is required first, an in-principle approval will be issued. Final approval will only be granted once documentation from other review(s) is provided.*
☐ None
☐ Yes, documentation attached
☐ Yes, documentation to follow (requires the University first)
Name of other boards/committees: *Provide the board name, address and contact information/person.*

SECTION 2: Research Project Information

Please complete each section below. Do not omit any questions.

9. Description of the Research Project: Use plain language to briefly describe the research project and its objectives (limit to one page.)

> The Rainbow Families Research Project is being headed by Family Services. The goal of this research is to obtain an overall demographic profile of LGBTTQ families in the XXX region. In addition, we would like to identify the unmet needs of children and youth of LGBTTQ parents, as well as the service needs of LGBTTQ families as a whole.
>
> The Rainbow Families Research Project will consist of the creation and implementation of an online survey, with separate sections of questions targeted to LGBTTQ family members and service providers.
>
> The outcomes of this research will be a clear picture of the demographics of LGBTTQ families in XXXX a comprehension of the needs of these families, and a gap analysis to identify needs that are not currently being met. The FS will use the research to expand upon existing programs or to create new programs to meet the identified needs.
>
> Family Services is dedicated to the health and well-being of all Ottawa families, offering programs and services to meet their needs.
>
> NOTE: LGBTTQ refers to those who identify themselves as lesbian, gay, bisexual, trans (including transsexual and transgendered), two-spirit and queer. LGBTTQ is the terminology generally recognized by this community in the XXXX region, and is the population in question for Family Services.

10. Methodology and Procedures:
a) The research requires the following from participants: (check all that apply)
☐ Brief survey/questionnaire (mail out or hand out)
☐ Brief survey/questionnaire conducted in person
☐ Brief interview (10-30 minutes)
☐ Long interview (over 30 minutes)
☐ More than one interview (several small or longer interviews)
☐ One interview with a follow-up to verify information
☐ Observations in workplace, home, etc.
☐ Participatory Action Project
☐ Accessing databases or files containing personal information
☐ Other: brief on-line survey

If more than one task is required please describe in what order they will take place.
n/a

Describe how long each procedure/task will take (minutes, hours and how many occasions and where the interview, procedure, testing, etc. will take place.)

> We estimate that the survey will take approximately 15-20 minutes, and will provide this estimate to participants at the beginning of the survey. Participants will only complete the survey once, and will be able to choose for themselves the time and place of survey completion. A copy of the survey has been included in this application, under SECTION 9.

11. Recruitment
Describe how participants will be identified and recruited.

> In order to obtain a large response rate, we will circulate a poster and supporting information to a large number of community organizations, groups, centres and resources. We are also planning to ask these organizations to post a link to the online survey on their own websites.
>
> The poster and supporting information will identify that participants should either be a member of an LGBTTQ family, or provide services, in the xxxx region.
>
> We also plan to advertise the survey further, using the social networking sites Facebook and Twitter. FS has an existing Facebook account, on which we will post the promotional poster for the survey. On both Facebook and Twitter, we will regularly

encourage people to take the survey. We will create a specific Twitter account for the survey, which will be deleted following the close of the survey. Neither site will be used to identify participants, or to promote discussion of the survey among potential participants. Both accounts will be monitored to ensure that participants are not identified in any way.

The planned promotional poster, Facebook and Twitter scripts have been included in this application, under SECTION 8.

Describe how contact with research participants will be made.

Contact with participants will be made solely through our promotion of the survey, as described above. Participants will self-select, and will complete the survey at a time and place of their own choosing.

Describe any relationship between yourself and the potential research participants (e.g., co-workers, fellow students, etc.)

Participants will remain anonymous throughout the research project. As such, it is impossible to determine any potential relationship between participants and members of the research team.

12. Exclusion criteria: (if any) Describe what criteria you will use to exclude potential participants and what steps you will take to inform participants that they do not qualify for the project.

The materials used in promoting the survey will identify that participants should either be a member of an LGBTTQ family, or provide services, in the XXXX region. A similar disclaimer will precede the beginning of the survey. In completing our analysis, the research team will consult the literature regarding accounting for false responses to online surveys.

13. Compensation:
Will participants receive compensation for their participation?
☐ Yes   ☐ No

If **Yes** describe the compensation (money, gift, transportation, childcare costs, etc.)

What is the monetary value of the compensation?

If participants withdraw what steps will you take to distribute the compensation?

14 Storage of data:

a) Describe where and how data will be stored during the research project.

> During the period of data collection, data will be stored on a secure server, as part of the online survey program, Survey Monkey (www.surveymonkey.com), and accessible only to research team members. Immediately following the close of data collection, the data will be deleted from this server and moved to a removable storage disk, again accessible only to research team members.

> It should be noted that, because Survey Monkey is a U.S.-based website, the data stored on the site may be accessed by the United States Government under the Patriot Act. Family Services is aware of this limitation to participants' confidentiality. Participants will also be made aware of this limitation to the survey's confidentiality during the consent process.

b) Describe how data will be stored at the conclusion of the project. If the data is to be destroyed indicate when and how?

> At the conclusion of the project, the data will be turned over to Family Services.

15 Dissemination: (Check all that apply)

☐ Thesis   ☐ Course research paper
☐ Academic journals   ☐ Web site/publication
☐ Book(s)   ☐ Workshops
☐ Conferences   ☐ Other:
☐ Classroom presentations/exercises

SECTION 3: Experience of researcher(s) with study population

16. Participants:

Participants are: (mark all that apply)

☐ Aboriginal peoples
☐ Immigrant groups
☐ Marginalized group
☐ Children (underage of 18)
☐ Senior citizens
☐ Incarcerated persons
☐ Professionals
☐ Patients or residents of a long-term care facility
☐ Other, specify: _____

Participants Gender: (mark all that apply)

☐ Male   ☐ Female   ☐ Transgendered

☐ Not applicable (ex. random sampling where gender is not an issue)

Number of participant's researchers plan on recruiting for this study:

> The number of participants is unknown, due to participant self-selection for an online survey.

Age range of participants:

> The age range for participants is unknown, due to participant self-selection for online survey.

NOTE: Participants under the age of 16 may require parental or legal guardian consent. In these cases submit a parent/legal guardian consent form.

Describe specific issues that need to be considered for the safe and ethical conduct of research with the selected research population. (i.e. matters of cultural and religious sensitivity, gender, language-barriers, and the collection of private and sensitive information.)

> Specific issues that were considered with the LGBTTQ population relate to the framing of the research results, emotional impact, anonymity and lack of coercion, language and privacy concerns. In terms of framing the data, every attempt was made to minimize misuse of the data. The issue of emotional impact is being addressed through the provision of information about a counselling service that is experienced in working with this population. This study offers anonymity as it is a self-select survey—to minimize the possibility of any participants feeling coerced. We will be using a self-administered online survey that ensures anonymity. In this way, people who wish to be excluded from the study will not fill out and return the survey. In terms of language, we will be careful in our promotion and analysis to use language that avoids the assumption that gender is binary, and is free of heterosexual bias.

17. Does the research involve vulnerable populations or distinct cultural groups?
☐ Yes   ☐ No

18. Describe your knowledge, training and experience working with this population and what steps you will take to ensure the safe, ethical conduct of research with the identified population.

> Researcher 1 has worked as an early childhood educator in a regulated licensed child care setting for numerous years with

young children and their families. Through the course of her work she has worked with many diverse families.

Researcher 2 has worked with members of the LGBTTQ population for numerous years in the areas of mental health counselling with adults and youth, and sexual assault counselling. She has a BA (Trent, 1990), and a Bachelor of Social Work (University of Manitoba, 2007) where she received training in human rights and issues relating to working with members of marginalized groups.

Researcher 3 has worked with diverse populations in social justice advocacy work, both in Canada and internationally. She holds a B.A. in history and political science (University of Toronto, 2005), and a Bachelor of Social Work (The University, 2009). She is also a member of an LGBTTQ family.

The steps we are taking to ensure the safe, ethical conduct of research with the identified population:

> prior to completing the online survey, participants will be informed of any potential privacy concerns,
> the design of the study allows participants to self- select, remain anonymous and to self-administer the survey,
> participants will be notified of counselling services experienced in working with the LGBTTQ community,
> promotion of the survey will not encourage discussion of the project,
> the research team will be careful to discuss the study's results "in ways that minimize the possibility that others could misuse them to harm the participants, the groups they represent, or those who serve them.
> data will be stored securely, as outlined in Section 2 (14).

SECTION 4: Conflict of Interest/Power Relationships

19. Are potential participants employees, clients or persons you have worked with in a volunteer capacity (past or present)?
☐ Yes   ☐ No

If **Yes** explain your relationship to or authority over the potential participants?

Are potential participants, friends, relatives or fellow students?
☐ Yes   ☐ No

If **Yes** explain why it is necessary to conduct research involving this population?

> Participants are from the xxxx Region. While it is possible that some participants may be friends, relatives or fellow students the research team will be unaware of this as it is a self-select online survey.

If **Yes** to either 4.1 or 4.2 describe what steps you will take to ensure that the participants' decision to take part in the research will not be influenced by their relationship to you.

SECTION 5: Description of Risks and Benefits

20. Risks to participants

☐ The risk to participants is minimal.

The following risks may exist: Check all that apply.

☐ Physical risk or discomfort (including any bodily contact, application of equipment, management of any substance.)

☐ Psychological risks (including feeling demeaned, embarrassed worried or upset, discussing personal sensitive information.)

☐ Social risks and economic risks (including possible loss of status, privacy and/or reputation, disclosure of sensitive information by others, possible loss of income, threat to employment.)

Explain all risks to participants. If you have described the project as minimal risk explain why it is minimal risk.

> The project is of minimal risk because participants self-select and self-administer the online survey. The survey questions are aimed at obtaining demographic information and quality services.

21. Managing risk: Explain what steps you will take to reduce the risk to participants.

> The demographic information we are collecting is non-identifying (i.e. first three letters of the participant's postal code), and participants may decline from answering any questions they do not want to answer. We are also asking participants if they have experienced discrimination when accessing services for themselves or their families, and how their families were formed. In the event that participants experience emotional distress as a result of participating in the survey, we are providing information on a counselling service that is experienced in working with members of the LGBTTQ community.

22. Deception: Is there any deception involved in this research project?

☐ Yes   ☐ No

If you answered Yes please describe why participants will be deceived, how it will carried out and how and when you will debrief participants.

23. Possible Benefits: Describe any potential or direct benefits to the participants from their involvement in the project. If there is no direct benefit to the participants clearly state so.

> Participants and the LGBTTQ community as a whole may benefit in the future if the project's results indicate a need for increased or more comprehensive services. Participants may directly benefit from their participation in the project through learning more about the individual and family services that are available to them in their community.

SECTION 6 – Anonymity and Confidentiality

24. Anonymity: Researchers treatment of the identity of participants
a) Will the identity of participants be known to researchers during the collection of information, data gathering or testing?
☐ Yes   ☐ No

b) Will the identity of participants be revealed in any reports, papers, research articles, presentations, etc?
☐ Yes   ☐ No

c) Will the identity of participants be known to other participants in the study?
☐ Yes   ☐ No

d) Will the identity of participants be known to non-participants in the study? (Example: colleagues, family friends of the participants)
☐ Yes   (at discretion of participant)   ☐   No

25. Confidentiality: Confidentiality refers to the non-attribution of data and responses.
The data collected will be anonymous and non-attributed to participants.
☐ Yes   ☐ No

The data collected will be attributed to participants.
☐ Yes   ☐ No

If you answered **Yes** to b): Will participants have the opportunity to request that certain responses remain non-attributable. ☐ Yes   ☐ No

26. Limitations on Confidentiality: If researchers anticipate any conflict between the research project procedures and data gathering and the law please describe those potential conflicts in detail.

Research and the law: There are legal limits on information researchers can promise to keep confidential. Example: child abuse and participants who may harm themselves or others. <u>Participants must be informed of these limitations as part of the consent process</u>.

> Because Survey Monkey is a U.S.-based website, the data stored on their server may be accessed by the United States Government under the Patriot Act. Family Services is aware of this limitation to participants' confidentiality. Participants will also be made aware of this limitation to the survey's confidentiality during the consent process.

27. Data Collection:
Will participants be audio recorded, photographed or video recorded?
☐ Yes   ☐ No

If **Yes**; describe what steps will be taken to secure the audio recordings during the course of the research. Explain your intentions to either save the recordings for future research or to destroy them. Explain how they will be destroyed.

b) Will the project require the services of a translator? ☐ Yes   ☐ No

If **Yes**; describe what steps will be taken to ensure the privacy and confidentiality of the participants. Attach a copy of the confidentiality agreement for the translator.

c) Will the project require a transcription service?   ☐ Yes   ☐ No
If **Yes**; describe what steps will be taken to ensure the privacy and confidentiality of the participants. Attach a copy of the confidentiality agreement for the transcription service.

SECTION 7: Informed Consent

29. Informed Consent Process
Describe the process that will be used to obtain informed consent.

> This research project will be a random sample online survey. It will be carried out as an on-line survey "SurveyMonkey" for both users and providers of services. Research participants will self-select. A disclaimer will be posted on the survey which reads, *"Disclaimer: The company that hosts this on-line survey "Survey Monkey" is located in the USA and is therefore subject to U.S laws including the US Patriot Act. The US Patriot Act gives the US Government greater access to electronic information including research databases"*. Informed consent will be assumed upon completion and return of the survey.

Are you seeking consent on behalf of a participant who is not legally or mentally competent to provide consent?　□ Yes　　　　□ No

If, **Yes** describe how you will address the potential power situation between the authorized party and the participant.

If there will be no written consent form, explain why.

> This is a random sample on-line survey. Research participants will self-select. A disclaimer will accompany the SurveyMonkey to inform participants wishing to take part that the host of the site is located in the US and subject to the US Patriot Act.

30. Participant withdrawal

Participants have the right to withdraw from a research project. Please explain the procedures for withdrawal. (Example: verbal or written notification from a participant.) If a participant cannot be withdrawn from the project explain why. (Example, random survey)

> This is a random sample online survey and consequently participants will only be identified by the three digit postal code. It will not be possible for the researchers to withdraw any of the surveys once submitted by the participant.

31. Participant feedback

Describe what feedback/information will be provided to participants after participation in the project. (For example, access to the results of the research).

> A report will be completed for Family Services and its partners in this project. They will be responsible for how they communicate the findings to services users and providers.

SECTION 8: Letters, Scripts & Consent Forms (Use the University letterhead)

Letter of Information, oral script, advertisement or poster: All required documents must be attached to the application as appendices. Please clearly mark each one (Example: Appendix 1: Letter of Information.) Please note that in some cases you will require more than one letter or script, such as when different groups participating in the same project have different tasks or risks, title each of these according to the participant group they are intended to address.

Consent form: Attach a copy of the informed consent form. In some cases the consent may be attached to the letter of information, in others it will be a separate document.

SECTION 9: Research Instrument

Attach copy of all research instruments for the project. This includes questionnaires, interview guides, sample questions, written tests and assignments, descriptions of apparatus and equipments.

SECTION 10: Supervision Plan (To be completed by supervisor)

Supervisors are responsible for overseeing a student's research ethics application and conduct throughout the project. The Committee requires the supervisor to explain the supervision plan for the student during the course of the research.

a) Frequency of meeting with student(s):

> The supervisor Karen Schwartz will meet weekly with the research team to review process.

b) Supervision of student during planned absences (sabbatical/researcher trips):

c) Date of the proposed thesis defence (if applicable):

SECTION 11: Signatures

Student Researcher(s):

Please indicate that you have read and fully understand all ethics obligations by checking the box beside each statement.

☐ I declare that the project information provided in this application is accurate.

☐ I agree to conduct the research in accordance with the *Tri-Council Policy Statement: Ethical Conduct for Research Involving Humans*, the *University Policies and Procedures for the Ethical Conduct of Research* and the conditions of approval established by the University Research Ethics Committee.

☐ I declare that during the course of this research I will be registered as a student at The University.

☐ I will report any serious adverse events to the Research Ethics Committee.

☐ I will submit additions or changes to the research project to the Research Ethics Committee.

☐ I agree to request a renewal of approval for any project continuing beyond the expected date of completion or for more than one year.

☐ I will submit a final report to the Research Ethics Committee once the research has been completed.

Signature _____ Date: _____

Signature _____ Date: _____

Signature _____ Date: _____

NOTE: All members of the researcher team are required to sign the application.

<u>Faculty Supervisor:</u>

Please indicate that you have read and fully understand the obligations as faculty supervisor listed below by checking the box beside each statement.

☐ I agree to provide the proper supervision of this study to ensure that the rights and welfare of all human participants are protected.
☐ I will ensure a request for renewal of a proposal is submitted if the study continues beyond the expected date of completion or for more than one year.
☐ I will ensure that a final report is submitted to the University Research Ethics Committee.
☐ I have read and approved the application and proposal.
Signature _____ Date: _____

Source: This example is from an actual project but identifying information has been deleted.

Appendix 4

Windsor Heights Community Asset Survey

1) How many people are in your home? _____

2) How many people in your home are 16 and older? _____

3) How many people in your home 16 and older are working:

	Full-Time	Part-time	Casual
Working			
Training			
Volunteering			

4) How many people 16 and older are attending school:

Vocational Training	
High School	
College	
University	

5) How many people 16 and older have completed:

Education Level	In Canada	Outside Canada
Vocational Training		
High School		
College		
University		
Masters		
Doctorate (PhD)		

6) How many people 16 and older are working in the area for which they were trained? _____

7) For those 16 and older that are unable to work in the area for which they were trained, please identify the barriers:

Education not recognized in Canada	
Lack of awareness/information on how to obtain Canadian certification	
Language	

Childcare	
Other:	
1,	
2.	
3.	

8)   What do you feel are the skills and talents of the people in your household? (examples: childcare, carpentry, cooking, musician, gardening)

a) _____

b)_____

c) _____

9)   Would you be willing to volunteer these skills and talents to the community?

Yes _____   No   _____

10) When you think about the Windsor Heights community, what are the three things you like best? (examples: supportive neighbours, community programs)

a) _____

b) _____

c) _____

11. What are three things that you feel could be improved in the Windsor Heights community? (examples: safety, maintenance)

a) _____

b) _____

c) _____

12. What are the languages spoken in your home?

_____ French   _____ Somali

_____ Arabic   _____ English

_____ Other

Source: Canteenwalla, Eagle, Phelps, and Zapotochny, 2006.

Writing Findings Section

(The following is an example of the findings section of one of our students'
final reports dealing with LGBTTQ families.)

2. Please tell us how your family was formed (i.e., how did your children
    come into your family?)

    We also asked LGBTTQ family members how their children came into
    their families. During the consultation process regarding the survey
    design, FSFO related that these stories would be important both
    for participants to tell, and for the research team to take into ac-
    count. Indeed, 29 of the 31 LGBTTQ family respondents answered this
    open-ended question, with a diversity of responses. Of this group,
    45% identified artificial insemination, whether through alternative
    insemination, anonymous donor or known or planned sperm donor.
    Another significant group, (34.5%), explained that their children
    came into their family from a previous heterosexual relationship.
    Five respondents (17%) adopted their children through Children's
    Aid Society (CAS). Two respondents (7%) had used both adoption
    and artificial insemination to bring children into their families. One
    respondent explained that she was a bisexual woman who had a
    child with a current male partner. Another respondent explained
    that she was seventy-five years old and the mother of a number of
    grown children and grandchildren.

3. Are there barriers for LGBTTQ families accessing services (i.e., cost, loca-
    tion, safety, childcare)? Please describe.

    When asked about the barriers to accessing services, 61% of LGBTTQ
    family members took the opportunity to tell their stories. Of the re-
    spondents who answered this open-ended question, 53% identified
    homophobia as a barrier for accessing services. In fact, only 19.4% of
    all LGBTTQ family member participants reported that they had never
    experienced discrimination when accessing services for their families.
    An additional 25.8% reported rarely experiencing discrimination,
    while 38.7% reported sometimes experiencing discrimination, and
    9.7% indicated that they often experience discrimination. One respon-
    dent reported experiencing discrimination very often. Participants
    who identified that they or someone in their family was trans reported
    much higher levels of discrimination than any other group.

    Similarly, only 22.6% of LGBTTQ family member participants felt that
    they and their families were consistently accepted by most services.
    A much larger portion of the participants felt accepted for the most
    part (41.9%) or somewhat accepted (32.3%) by most services. When
    asked if most services they use respect LGBTTQ families, only 12.9%

felt that their families were consistently respected by services. Again, most felt that their families were respected only for the most part (45.2%) or somewhat (32.3%). One participant indicated that most services did not respect LGBTTQ families at all.

It should be noted that users of certain types of services were more likely to report experiencing discrimination than users of other services. LGBTTQ family members who accessed parenting courses and counseling services reported experiencing higher levels of discrimination, while those who accessed educational services reported the lowest levels of discrimination. LGBTTQ family members also indicated lower levels of respect for LGBTTQ families among parenting courses and counseling services; the highest levels of respect were reported by families accessing health and recreational services. Counseling services also scored lower in terms of acceptance of LGBTTQ families, while families using health and recreational services reported the highest levels of acceptance for their families.

Participants identified the nature of the discrimination experienced in "agencies not acknowledging family types other than traditional nuclear families." Two respondents expressed that they were not accepted as the legitimate mothers of their non-biological children. One explained, "Once staff meets one mother, they don't expect there to be a second and so I am often ignored." Another participant explained that they were "fearful that the children would suffer homophobic remarks or attitudes if they were open about being a LGBTTQ family." Two respondents identified trans-phobia as a problem, and reported that there are not enough services and supports specifically for trans-families. Interestingly, one trans participant explained, "Being a trans-parent meant that many services providers take me as a female and my family as a typical heterosexual family." In this way, discrimination is experienced as a lack of knowledge about the needs of trans families.

One participant explained that while she had not directly experienced homophobia, the conventional representation of mainstream heterosexual families and parents within agency settings is limiting and acts as a barrier for LGBTTQ families. Another respondent echoed the difficulty of being a nuclear family within the LGBTTQ community and the feeling of "living apart." One participant explained that "preschool programs and recreation programs in the main assume that kids come from 2-parent heterosexual families." Another expressed frustration with having to explain her family structure "over and over again." A fellow participant lamented "constantly having to educate services providers about our family before being able to access services."

Two LGBTTQ family members raised the point that external and internalized homophobia in education and in the medical field impacts on their ability to access services, and on their children's experience of services. Direct forms of discrimination were identified. One participant wrote, "We and our children were the focus of anti-gay comments at school functions and the kids were bullied in both the Catholic and Public schools." Another respondent described, "We did run into one incident where the non-biological parent's relationship to our daughter was questioned at the hospital."

Service providers also identified homophobia, "lack of sensitivity to the needs of LGBTTQ individuals, lack of knowledge of the discrimination and barriers faced by LGBTTQ individuals, lack of understanding," stigmatization, fear of stigma, lack of sensitivity training for working with the transgender community, and lack of resources as barriers to effective services for LGBTTQ families. The lack of specialized training, insufficient services for LGBTTQ families and not all "LGBTTQ families feeling a sense of belonging to the community" were also noted. One service provider expressed the opinion that "Service providers that do not identify as LGBTTQ should not be in a leadership role. Counselors, front-line staff, and management should all include individuals who are members of the [LGBTTQ] community." Service providers identified heterosexism in the ways in which services usually do not affirm LGBTTQ family structure, in how partner abuse services rarely address abuse in same-sex relationships, and in how parenting course are primarily attended by heterosexual couples.

Six (31%) of the LGBTTQ family members responding to the open-ended question regarding barriers to service reported that cost, time or location acted as barriers to accessing services. In particular, cost was cited specifically by four respondents. One participant wrote about the difficulty of finding services for LGBTTQ families in rural and small town settings, as well as the hardship of having to travel a distance to access the kinds of services the family needed. Three respondents identified that being unable to access child care was a barrier for them to take part in support programs and counseling. One explained, "Child care is a constant barrier — we would take advantage of many more services and activities if we had low-cost, reliable child care." Two LGBTTQ family members indicated that the times that programs and services were available posed a challenge for them.

Finally, 26% of LGBTTQ family members responding to the open-ended question regarding barriers to service access wrote that there are not enough dedicated courses, programs or services for children of LGBTTQ parents, and that there are insufficient services for older children of LGBTTQ families. One respondent observed that some families feel isolated and unsure of where to go for help. Another indicated that "it would be great to have more support groups for LGBTTQ families dealing with difficult issues."

Source: Shannon Sommerauer, Kate Hanton, Shellie Bird, Around the Rainbow Project Report, March 31, 2010.

Bibliography

Agyei-Amoama, A., J. Ashley, A. Layiki-Dehne, N. MacDonald, M. O'Donnell and Y. Zeng. 2008. "Uncovering Barriers and Identifying Pathways to Educational Success for African and Caribbean Youth in Ottawa." Unpublished paper.

Ahmed. S.M., B. Beck, C.A. Murana and G. Newton. 2004. "Overcoming Barriers to Effective Community-Based Participatory Research in U.S. Medical Schools." *Education For Health* 17 (2): 141–51.

Alinsky, S. 1969. *Reveille for Radicals.* New York: Vintage Books.

Anderson, S. 2002. "Engaging Students in Community-Based Research: A Model for Teaching Social Work Research." *Journal of Community Practice* 10 (2).

Andree, P. (2008). "Community-Based Research as Pedagogy: Learning to Put Theory into Practice in the Undergraduate Classroom." In Darlene E. Clover and Catherine McGregor (eds.), *Community-University Partnerships: Connecting for Change — Proceedings of the Third International Community-University Exposition* (CUexpo 2008), Victoria, BC: University of Victoria.

Annett, K.D. 1998. *Hidden from History: The Canadian Holocaust.* Third edition. The Truth Commission into Genocide in Canada.

Arches, J. 2007. "Youth Take Charge: Social Action in a Community-University Partnership." In N.G. Hofman and H. Rosing (eds.), *Pedagogies of Praxis: Course-based Research in the Social Sciences.* Boston, MA: Anker Publishing.

Baines, D. (ed.). 2007. *Doing Anti-Oppressive Practice: Building Transformative Politicized Social Work.* Halifax/Winnipeg: Fernwood Publishing.

Balcazar, F.E., E. Garcia-Iriarte and Y. Suarez-Balcazar. 2009. "Participatory Action Research With Colombian Immigrants." *Hispanic Journal of Behavioral Sciences* 31.

Baum, F., C. MacDougall and D. Smith. 2006. "Participatory Action Research." *Journal of Epidemiology and Community Health* 60 (10): 854–57.

Bennett, M. 2004. "A review of the Literature on the Benefits and Drawbacks of Participatory Action Research." *First Nations Child and Family Review* 1 (1).

Berg, B. 2007. *Qualitative Research Methods for the Social Sciences.* Sixth edition. Montreal, PQ: Pearson Education.

_____. 2004. *Qualitative Research Methods for the Social Sciences.* Fifth edition. Montreal, PQ: Pearson Education.

Bird, S.E., J.P. Ambiee and J. Kuzin. 2007. "Action Research in a Visual Anthropology Class: Lessons, Frustrations and Achievements." In N.G. Hofman and H. Rosing (eds.), *Pedagogies of Praxis: Course-Based Research in the Social Sciences.* Boston: Anker Publishing.

Blackstock, C. 2009. "The Occasional Evil of Angels: Learning from the Experiences of Aboriginal Peoples and Social Work." *First Nations Child and Family Review* 4 (1).

Bogo, M. 2006. *Social Work Practice: Concepts, Processes and Interviewing.* New York, NY: Columbia University Press.

Boser, S. 2006. "Ethics and Power in Community-Campus Partnerships for Research." *Action Research* 4 (1).

Brascoupe, S., and H. Mann. 2001. *A Community Guide to Protecting Indigenous Knowledge.* Ottawa: Research and Analysis Directorate, Department of Indian and Northern Development.

Brown, L., and M. Reitsma-Street. 2003. "The Values of Community Action Research." *Canadian Journal of Social Work Education* 20 (1).

Brun, C. 2005. *Social Service Evaluation: A Practical Guide.* Chicago, IL: Lyceum Books.

Bryman, A., and J.J. Teevan. 2005. *Social Research Methods.* Canadian edition. Toronto, ON: Oxford University Press.

Bzruzy, S., and E.A. Segal. 1996. "Community-Based Research Strategies for Social Work Education. *Journal of Community Practice* 3 (1).

Canadian Council on Children and Youth. 1978. *Admittance Restricted: The Child as Citizen in Canada.* Ottawa, ON: Canadian Council on Children and Youth.

Canteenwalla, Z., B. Eagle, F. Phelps and T. Zapotochny. 2006. "Assessing Community Capacity in Russell Heights Community." Ottawa: Carleton University (unpublished).

CASW-ACTS. 2005. "CASW Code of Ethics and Guidelines for Ethical Behaviour." <http://www.casw-acts.ca/>.

CASWE-ACFTS. 2008. "Standards of Accreditation." <www.caswe-acfts.ca/en-Board-of-accreditation.http://www.caswe-acfts.ca/vm/newvisual/attachments/866/Media/StandardsofAccreditationMay200825012010sl.pdf>.

Chapdelaine, A., and B.L. Chapman. 1999. "Using Community-Based Research Projects to Teach Research Methods." *Teaching of Psychology* 26 (2).

Cohen, E., and J. Angeles. 2006. "School-Based Prevalence Assessment of the Need for Mental Health Services: Survey Development and Pilot Study." *Research on Social Work Practice* 16 (2).

Comeau, P., and A. Santin. 1995. *The First Canadians: A Profile of Canada's Native People Today.* Toronto, ON: James Lorimer.

Compton, B., and B. Gallaway. 1999. *Social work Processes.* Sixth edition. Pacific Grove, CA: Brooks/Cole – Thompson Learning.

Deegan. M.J. 1988. *Jane Addams and the Men of the Chicago School, 1892–1918.* New Brunswick: Transaction, Inc.

Dickason, O.P. 1992. *Canada's First Nations: A History of Founding Peoples from Earliest Times.* Toronto, ON: McClelland and Stewart.

Dudley, J. 2010. *Research Methods for Social Work: Being Producers and Consumers of Research.* Second edition. Boston, MA: Pearson Education.

_____. 2009. *Social Work Evaluation: Enhancing What We Do.* Chicago, IL: Lyceum Books.

Dyck, E. 2005. "Flashback: Psychiatric Experimentation with LSD in Historical Perspective." *Canadian Journal of Psychiatry* 50 (7): 381–88.

England, H. 1986. *Social Work as Art: Making Sense for Good Practice.* London, ON:

Allen and Unwin.

Etmanski C., and M. Pant. 2007. "Teaching Participatory Research through Reflexivity and Relationship." *Action Research* 5 (3).

Everrett, T. 2007. *Hearing Our Voices: A Participatory Research Study on Schizophrenia and Homelessness.* Video recording. Calgary, AB: University of Calgary.

Eyler, J., D. Giles, C.M. Stenson and C.J. Gray. 2001. *At a Glance: What we Know about the Effects of Service Learning on College Students. Faculty Institutions and Communities, 1993–2000.* Third edition. Nashville, TN: Vanderbilt University.

Fals-Borda, O., and M.A. Rahman (eds.). 1991. *Action and Knowledge: Breaking the Monopoly with Participatory Action Research.* New York, NY: Apex Press.

Faulkner, C.A., and S.S. Faulkner. 2009. *Research Methods for Social Workers.* Chicago, IL: Lyceum Books.

Fischer, J. 2009. *Toward Evidence-Based Practice: Variations on a Theme.* Chicago, IL: Lyceum Books.

_____. 1976. *The Effectiveness of Social Casework.* Springfield, IL: Charles G. Thomas.

Flicker, S. 2008. "Who Benefits from Community-Based Participatory Research? A Case Study of the Positive Youth Project." *Health Education and Behavior* 35 (1).

Flicker, S., and B. Savan. 2006. *A Snapshot of CBR in Canada.* Wellesley Institute. <http://www.uvic.ca/research/ocbr/assets/pdfs/CBR_snapshot_report_final. pdf>.

Flicker, S., B. Savan, M. Mc Grath, B. Kolenda and M. Mildenberger. 2007. "'If You Could Change One Thing...' What Community-Based Researchers Wish They Could Have Done Differently." *Community Development Journal* 43 (2).

Fook, J. 1996. *The Reflective Researcher: Social Worker's Theories of Practice Research.* St. Leonards: Allen and Unwin.

Fox, M., P. Martin and G. Green. 2007. *Doing Practitioner Research.* London: Sage Publications.

Freire, P. 2005. *Pedagogy of the Oppressed.* New York, NY: Continuum.

_____. 1985. *The Politics of Education: Culture, Power and Liberation.* South Hadley, MA: Bergin & Garvey Publishers.

Gilchrist, L. 1999. "Aboriginal Communities and Social Science Research: Voyeurism in Transition." *Native Social Work Journal* 1 (1).

Gregg, R. 1994. "Exploration of Pregnancy and Choice in a High Tech Age." In C.K. Reissman (ed.), *Qualitative Studies in Social Work Research.* Thousand Oaks, CA: Sage Publications.

Grinnell, M., M. Williams and Y.A. Unrau. 2009. *Research Methods for BSW Students.* Eighth edition. Kalamazoo, MI: Pair Bond Publications.

Grinnel, R.M., and Y.A. Unrau. 2011. *Social Work Research and Evaluation: Foundations of Evidence-Based Practice.* New York, NY: Oxford University Press.

Hall, Budd L. 2005. "In From the Cold: Reflections on Participatory Research from 1970–2005." *Convergence* 38 (1).

Hammers, C., and A.D. Brown. 2004. "Towards a Feminist-Queer Alliance: A Paradigmatic Shift in the Research Process." *Social Epistemology* 18 (1).

Harding, S. 1987. "Conclusion: Epistemological Questions." In S. Harding (ed.), *Feminism and Methodology.* Bloomington, IN: Indian University Press.

Hartsock, N. 1983. "The Feminist Standpoint: Develping the Ground for a

Specifically Feminist Historical Materialism." In S. Harding and M.B. Hintika (eds.), *Discovering Reality*. London, UK: D. Reiel Publishing.

Hauck, Y., D. Rock, T. Jackiewicz and A. Jablensky. 2008. "Healthy Babies for Mothers with Serious Mental Illness: A Case Management Framework for Mental Health Clinicians." *International Journal of Mental Health Nursing* 17.

Hayes, E. 2006. "Community Service Learning in Canada: A Scan of the Field." <http:www.communityservicelearning.ca>.

Heinonen, T., and L. Spearman. 2001. *Social work Practice: Problem Solving and Beyond*. Toronto, ON: Irwin Publishing.

Hepworth, P. 1980. *Foster Care and Adoption in Canada*. Ottawa: Canadian Council on Social Development.

Herbert, M., and K. Harper-Dorton. 2002. *Working with Children, Adolescents, and Their Families*. Third edition. Chicago, IL: Lyceum Books.

Hick, S. 1997. "Participatory Research: An Approach for Structural Social Workers." *Journal of Progressive Human Services* 8 (2).

Hudson, C.G. 2005. "Socioeconomic Status and Mental Illness: Tests of the Social Causation and Selection Hypotheses." *American Journal of Orthopsychiatry* 75 (1).

Hyde, C.A., and M. Meyer. 2004. "A Collaborative Approach to Service, Learning, and Scholarship: A Community-Based Research Course." *Journal of Community Practice* 12 (1/2).

Ibanez-Carrasco, F. 2004. "CBR: Luxury or Necessity? An Environmental Scan of the British Columbia Community Based Research Capacity Building Needs, Capacities and Challenges." Paper prepare for British Columbia Persons with AIDS Society.

Jackson, T. 1993. "'A Way of Working: Participatory Research and the Aboriginal Movement in Canada." In P. Park, M. Brydon-Miller, B. Hall and T. Jackson (eds.), *Voices of Change: Participatory Research in the United States and Canada*. Toronto, ON: OISE Press.

Jamil, H., M.S.C. Nassar and R.G. Lambert. 2007. "Immigration and Attendant Psychological Sequelae: A Comparison of Three Waves of Iraqi Immigrants." *American Journal of Orthopsychiatry* 77 (2).

Jenkins, M.A. 2003. "Young Single Mother and Welfare Reform." *Journal of Child and Youth Care Work* 18. Milwaukee: University of Wisconsin-Milwaukee and Concordia University.

Jenkins, M.A., and M. Hagi-Aden. 2008. "What Makes It Ours: Lessons Learned from the Our Place-Learning in Motion Initiative." Unpublished report. Ottawa: South-East Ottawa Community Health Centre.

Johnson, R., and A. Rounce. 2007. "Universities and Community Engagement: New Directions for the 'Third Mission'." In B. Dern and C. Stoney (eds.), *Universities in the Knowledge-Based Economy: Policy, Regulation and Innovation*. Toronto, ON: University of Toronto Press.

Johnston. P. 1983. *Native Children and the Child Welfare System*. Toronto, ON: Canadian Council on Social Development and James Lorimer and Company.

Kindon, S., R. Pain and M. Kesby. 2007. *Participatory Action Research Approaches and Methods: Connecting People, Participation and Place*. London, UK: Routledge.

Kirby, M.J.L., and W.J. Keon. 2006. "Out of the Shadows at Last: Transforming Mental Health, Mental Illness and Addiction Services in Canada." Final report of the Standing Senate Committee on Social Affairs, Science and Technology.

Kirby, S., L. Greaves and C. Reid. 2006. *Experience Research Social Change: Methods Beyond the Mainstream.* Second edition. Peterborough, ON: Broadview Press.

Kreuger, L., and W. Neuman. 2006. S*ocial Work Research Methods: Qualitative and Quantitative Applications.* Boston: Pearson Education.

Kuhn, T.S. 1970. *The Structure of Scientific Revolutions.* Chicago: University of Chicago.

Lai, Y., L. Forster, C. Head, A. Helfer and R. Fuchs. 2008. "Assessing Community Capacity." Unpublished research project.Ottawa: Carleton University.

Lavoie, C., J. MacDonald and B. Whitmore. 2010. "Methods for Understanding, Learning and Social Justice." In I. Shaw, K. Briar-Lawson, J. Orme, and R. Ruckdeschel (ed.), *The Sage Handbook of Social Work Research.* Thousand Oaks: CA, Sage Publications.

Leavy, P. 2009. *Method Meets Art: Arts-Based Research Practice.* New York, NY: Guilford Press.

Lertherby, G. 2003. *Feminist Research in Theory and Practice.* Buckingham, U.K.: Open University Press.

Lincoln, Y., and E. Guba. 1985. *Naturalistic Inquiry.* Beverly Hills, CA: Sage Publications.

Longino, H. 1990. *Science as Social Knowledge.* Princeton, NJ: Princeton University Press.

Lundy, C. 2004. *Social Work and Social Justice.* Peterborough, ON: Broadview Press.

Manderscheid, R.W. 2006. "Some Thoughts on the Relationships between Evidence Based Practices, Practice Based Evidence, Outcomes, and Performance Measures." *Administrative Policy Mental Health and Mental Health Services* 33 (6).

Margolin, L. 1997. *Under the Cover of Kindness: The Invention of Social Work.* Charlottesville, VA: University Press of Virginia.

Marlow, C. 2005. *Research Methods for Generalist Social Work.* Fourth edition. Pacific Grove, CA: Brooks/Cole Publishing.

McDonald, M.A. 2007. *Practicing Community-Engaged Research.* Duke University Medical Center Research Ethics. <http://researchethics.nc.duke.edu>.

McGoldrick, M., R. Gerson and S. Shellenberger. 1999. *Genograms: Assessment and Intervention.* Second edition. New York, NY: W.W. Norton.

McKenzie, B., and P. Hudson. 1985. "Native Children, Child Welfare, and the Colonization of Native People." In K.L. Levitt, and B. Wharf (eds.), *The Challenge of Child Welfare.* Vancouver, BC: University of British Columbia Press.

Menzies, P., and A. van de Sande. 2003. "A Formative Evaluation of the Customary Care Program: Native Child and Family Services of Toronto." *Native Social Work Journal* 4 (1).

Middleman, R.R., and G. Goldberg. 1974. *Social Service Delivery: A Structural Approach to Social Work Practice.* New York, NY: Columbia University Press.

Milgram, S. 1983. *Obedience to Authority.* Harper Perennial.

Minkler, M. 2005. "Community-Based Research Partnerships: Challenges and Opportunities." *Journal of Urban Health* 82 (2).

_____. 2004. "Ethical Challenges for the Outside Researcher in Community-Based Participatory Research." *Health Education and Behavior* 31 (6).

Moore, P. 2008. "Reflexive Journal, SOWK 5405." Unpublished paper.

Moreau, M. 1989. *Empowerment through a Structural Approach: A Report for Practice.* Ottawa, ON: Carleton University.

_____. 1979. "A Structural Approach to Social Work Practice." *Canadian Journal of Social Work Education* 5 (1).

Moretti, M., B. Leadbeater and A. Marshall. 2006. "Stepping into Community-Based Research: Preparing Students to Meet New Ethical and Professional Challenges." In B. Leadbeater, E. Banister, C. Benoit, M. Jansson, A. Marshall and T. Riecken (eds.), *Ethical Issues in Community-Based Research with Children and Youth.* Toronto, ON: University of Toronto Press.

Mullaly, B. 2007. *The New Structural Social Work.* Third edition. Toronto, ON: Oxford University Press.

_____. 1997. *Structural Social Work: Ideology, Theory, and Practice.* Second edition. Toronto, ON: Oxford University Press.

_____. 1993. *Structural Social Work: Ideology, Theory, and Practice.* Toronto, ON: Oxford University Press.

Mulroy, E.A. 2004. "University Civic Engagement with Community-Based Organizations: Dispersed or Coordinated Model." In T. Soska and A. J. Butterfield (eds.), *University-Community Partnerships: Universities in Civic Engagement.* Haworth Social Work Practice Press, Haworth Press.

Nardi, P.M. 2003. *Doing Survey Research: A Guide to Quantitative Methods.* Boston, MA: Pearson Education.

NASW. 2008. "National Association of Social Work Code of Ethics." <http://www.naswdc.org/pubs/code/code.asp>.

National Biomedical Research Fellowship, Traineeship, and Training Act. 1974. Public Law 93-348.

Nelson, G., R. Janzen, J. Trainor and J. Ochocka. 2008. "Putting Values into Practice: Public Policy and the Future of Mental Health Consumer-Run Organizations." *American Journal of Community Psychology* 42.

Nelson, K., K. Schwartz and A. van de Sande. 2009. "Social Work Research in Action: Building Partnerships: Opportunities and Challenges." Paper presented at Social Work Research Day.

Neuman, L., and K. Robson. 2009. *Basics of Social Research: Qualitative and Quantitative Approaches.* Toronto, ON: Pearson Education.

Neuman, W.L. 2006. *Social Research Methods: Qualitative and Quantitative Approaches.* Sixth edition. Boston, MA: Pearson Education.

Neuman, W.L., and L.W. Kreuger. 2003. *Social Work Research Methods: Qualitative and Quantitative Methods.* Montreal: Pearson Education.

Norton, I.M., and S.M. Manson. 1996. "Research in American Indian and Alaska Native Communities: Navigating the Cultural Universe of Values and Process." As cited in A. Rubin and E.R. Babbie (eds.), 2010, *Essential Research Methods for Social Work.* Second edition. Belmont, CA: Books/Cole.

O'Hare, T. 2005. *Evidence-Based Practices for Social Workers: An Interdisciplinary Approach.* Chicago, IL: Lyceum Books.

Ottawa Ministry website. n.d. <http://www.ottawamission.com/index.php?q=hospice.html>.

Padgett, D.K. 2008. *Qualitative Methods in Social Work Research.* Second edition.

Thousand Oaks, CA: Sage Publications.

_____. 2004. *The Qualitative Research Experience*. Belmont, CA: Thomson Brooks/ Cole.

Patton, M.Q. 1978. *Utilization-Focused Evaluation*. Beverly Hills, CA: Sage.

Payne, M. 2005. *Modern Social Work Theory*. Chicago, IL: Lyceum Books.

Pease, B. 2000. *Recreating Men: Postmodern Masculinity Politics*. London, UK: Sage Publications.

Peters, J.M., and A. Gray. 2007. "Teaching and Learning in a Model-Based Action Research Course." *Action Research* 5 (3).

Prilleltensky, I. 2001. "Value-Based Praxis in Community Psychology: Moving Towards Social Justice and Social Action." *American Journal of Community Psychology* 29.

Ray, A. 1996. *I Have Lived Here since the World Began: An Illustrated History of Canada's Native People*. Toronto, ON: Lester Publications.

Reasons, C.E., and W.D. Perdue. 1981. *Ideology of Social Problems*. Scarborough, ON: Nelson Canada.

Regehr, C., and K. Kanani. 2010. *Essential Law for Social Work Practice*. Second edition. Don Mills, ON: Oxford University Press.

Renzetti, C.M., and R.M. Lee (eds.). 1993. *Researching Sensitive Topics*. London, UK: Sage Publications.

Richardson, L. 1990. *Writing Strategies: Reaching Diverse Audiences*. London, UK: Sage Publications.

Ristock, J.L., and J. Pennell. 1996. *Community Research as Empowerment: Feminist Links, Postmodern Interruptions*. Toronto, ON: Oxford University Press.

Robson, C. 1993. *Real World Enquiry: A Resource for Social Scientists and Practitioner-Researchers*. As quoted in M. Walter, 2006, "Participatory Action Research," Chapter 21, *Social Research Methods*. Oxford, UK: Blackwell.

Rogge, M.E., and C.J. Rocha. 2004. "University-Community Partnership Centers: An Important Link for Social Work Education." *Journal of Community Practice* 12 (3–4).

Rosenberg, M. 1965. *Society and the Adolescent Self-Image*. Princeton, NJ: Princeton University Press.

Rossiter, A. 2000. "The Postmodern Feminist Condition: New Conditions for Social Work." In B. Fawcett, B. Featherstone, J. Fook and A. Rossiter (eds.), *Practice and Research in Social Work: Postmodern Feminist Perspectives*. London, UK: Routledge.

Rothman, J. 1979. "Three Models of Community Organization Practice, Their Mixing and Phasing." In F. Cox et al. (eds.), *Strategies of Community Organization*. Third edition. Itasca, IL: F.E. Peacock.

Royse, D. 2008. *Research Methods in social Work*. Fifth edition. Belmont, CA: Books/ Cole.

Rubin, A., and E.R. Babbie. 2010. *Essential Research Methods for Social Work*. Second edition. Belmont, CA: Books/Cole.

_____. 2008. *Research Methods for Social Work*. Sixth edition. Belmont, CA: Thompson Higher Education.

Saleeby, D. 2002. *The Strengths Perspective in Social Work Practice*. Third edition. Boston, MA: Allyn and Bacon.

Savan, B. 2004. "Community-University Partnerships: Linking Research and Action for Sustainable Community Development." *Community Development Journal* 39: 4.

Schwartz, K. 2010. "Community Engaged Research: Student and Community Perspectives." *Partnerships: A Journal of Service-Learning and Civic Engagement* 1 (2).

Schwartz, K., and M. O'Brien. 2010. "Injustice Can Happen Whether You're Psychotic or Not: Incorporating Structural Social Work Theory in a Mental Health Setting." In S. Hick, H. Peters, T. Corner and T. London (eds.), *Structural Social Work in Action: Examples From Practice*. Toronto, ON: Canadian Scholars Press.

Schwartz, K., A-M. O'Brien and A. van de Sande. 2009. "Building Collaborative Relationships for Student Engagement Between Schools of Social Work and Mental Health Care Settings." Paper presented at International Partnership Institute: Reciprocal Partnerships: Transforming Higher Education and Community for the Future, Portland, Oregon.

Schwartz, K., and A. van de Sande. 2008. "The Third Responsibility: Students Contributing to the Community by Engaging in Community Based Research." In D.E. Clover and C. McGregor (eds.), *Community-University Partnerships: Connecting for Change: Proceedings of the Third International Community-University Exposition* (CUexpo 2008), University of Victoria.

Seifer, S.D. 2006. "Building and Sustaining Community-Institutional Partnerships for Prevention Research: Findings from a National Collaborative." Corporate author: Examining Community-Institutional Partnerships for Prevention Research Group. *Journal of Urban Health-Bulletin of the New York Academy of Medicine* 83 (6).

Seifer, S.D., and D.C. Calleson. 2004. "Health Professional Faculty Perspectives on Community-Based Research: Implications for Policy and Practice." *Journal of Interprofessional Care* 18 (4).

Sheafor, B.W., C.R. Horejsi and G.A. Horejsi. 1991. *Techniques and Guidelines for Social Work Practice*. Second edition. Boston, MA: Allyn and Bacon.

Shiu-Thornton, S. 2003. "Addressing Cultural Competency in Research: Integrating a Community-Based Participatory Research Approach." *Alcoholism, Clinical and Experimental Research* 27 (8).

Shulman, L. 1999. *The Skills of Helping Individuals, Families, Groups and Communities*. Fourth edition. Itasca, IL: F.E. Peacock.

Sin, R. 2007. "Community Action Research: lessons from the Chinese Communities in Montreal." In D. Baines (ed.), *Doing Anti-Oppressive Practice: Building Transformative Politicized Social Work*. Halifax, NS: Fernwood Publishing.

Sinclair, R. 2004. "Aboriginal Social Work Education: Decolonizing Pedagogy for the Seventh Generation." *First Nations Child and Family Review* 1 (1).

Smith, D. 1987. *The Everyday World as Problematic: A Feminist Sociology*. Milton Keynes: Open University Press.

Smith, L.T. 1999. *Decolonizing Methodologies: Research and Indigenous Peoples*. London, UK: Zed Books.

Stanton, T.K. 2008. "New Times Demand New Scholarship: Opportunities and Challenges for Civic Engagement." *Education, Citizenship and Social Justice* 3.

Stoecker, R. 2003. "Community-Based Research: From Practice to Theory and Back Again." *Michigan Jounal of Community Service Learning* 9 (2): 35–46.

Strand, K. 2000. "Community-Based Research as Pedagogy." *Michigan Journal of Community Service Learning* 7: 85–96.

Strand, K., S. Marullo, N. Cutforth, R. Stoecker and P. Donohue. 2003a. "Principles of best practice for community-based research." *Michigan Journal of Community Service Learning* 9 (3).

_____. 2003b. *Community-Based Research and Higher Education*. San Francisco: Jossey-Bass.

Strega, S., and S. Aski-Esquao. 2009. Walking the Path Together: Ant-Racist and Anti-Oppressive Child Welfare Practice. Halifax, NS: Fernwood Publishing.

Stuart, C., and E. Whitmore. 2006. "Using Reflexivity in a Research Methods Course: Bridging the Gap between Research and Practice." In S. White, J. Fook and F. Gardner (eds.), *Critical Reflection in Health and Social Care*. Berkshire, UK, Open University Press.

Sullivan, M., A. Kone, K.D. Senturia, N.J. Chrisman, S.J. Ciske and J.W. Kreiger. 2001. "Researcher and Researched-Community Perspectives: Toward Bridging the Gap." *Health Education and Behaviour* 28 (2).

Tanesini, A. 1999. *An Introduction to Feminist Epistemologies*. Malden, MA: Blackwell Publishers.

Thiessen, V. 1993. *Arguing with Numbers: Statistics for the Social Sciences*. Halifax, NS: Fernwood Publishing.

Toseland, R.W., and R.F. Rivas. 1998. *Introduction to Group Work Practice*. Boston, MA: Allyn and Bacon.

Transken, S. 2002. "Poetically Teaching/Doing the Profession of Social Work as a Joyful UnDisciplined Discipline-Jumper and Genre-Jumper." *Critical Social Work* 3 (1). <http://www.uwindsor.ca/criticalsocialwork/2002-volume-3-no-1>.

Tri-Council. 2005. *Tri-Council Policy Statement: Ethical Conduct for Research Involving Human Subjects*. Ottawa: Government of Canada. <http://www.ethics.gc.ca/pdf/eng/tcps2/TCPS_2_FINAL_Web.pdf>

Trinder, L. 2000. "Reading the Texts: Postmodern Feminism and the 'Doing' of Research." In B. Fawcett, B. Featherstone, J. Fook and Amy Rossiter (eds.), *Practice and Research in Social Work: Postmodern Feminist Perspectives*. London, UK: Routledge.

Tutty, L., M. Rothery and R. Grinnell. 1996. *Qualitative Research for Social Workers*. Boston, MA: Allyn and Bacon.

van de Sande, A., and P. Menzies. 2003. Native and Mainstream Parenting: A Comparative Study. *Native Social Work Journal* 4 (1).

Wadsworth, Y. 2006. "The Mirror, the Magnifying Glass, the Compass and the Map: Facilitating PAR." In P. Reqason and H. Bradbury (eds.), *Handbook of Action Research*. London, UK: Sage.

_____. 1998. "What Is Participatory Action Research?" Paper 2. Action Research International. <http://www.scu.edu.au/schools/gcm/ar/ari/p-ywadsworth98.html>.

Weinbach, R., and R.M. Grinnell. 2007. *Statistics for Social Workers*. Seventh edition. Boston, MA: Pearson Education.

Weinberg, M. 2010. "The Social Construction of Social Work Ethics: Politicizing and Braidening the Lens." *Journal of Progressive Human Services* 21.

Westhues, A., S. Cadell, J. Karabanow, L. Maxwell and M. Sanchez. 1999. "The

Creation of Knowledge: Linking Research Paradigms to Practice." *Canadian Social Work Review* 16 (2).

Wilson, S. 2008. *Research Is Ceremony: Indigenous Research Methods.* Halifax, NS: Fernwood Publishing.

Yegidis, B., R. Weinbach and B. Morrison-Rodriquez. 2009. *Research Methods for Social Workers.* Sixth edition. Boston, MA: Allyn and Bacon.

Yin, R.K. 2011. *Qualitative Research from Start to Finish.* New York, NY: Guilford Press.

Yohani, S.C. 2008. "Creating an Ecology of Hope: Arts-Based Interventions with Refugee Children." *Child and Adolescent Social Work Journal* 25 (4).

Index